IMAGES, MEANINGS AND CONNECTIONS

Essays in Memory of Susan R. Bach

Images, Meanings and Connections

Essays in Memory of Susan R. Bach

Edited by Ralph Goldstein

DAIMON

We wish to express our heartfelt gratitude to the Omega Foundation, London,
for their generous support of this project.

ISBN 3-85630-586-6

Contents

8

Acknowledgements

I am very grateful to all those who encouraged me in the editing of this memorial volume and in this connection, I am particularly grateful to Dr. Christopher Donovan, Chair of the Omega Foundation, London, and to Dr. Robert Hinshaw of Daimon Verlag. Robert has been more of a supportive colleague and friend than a publisher, since we worked together with Susan Bach in seeing *Life Paints Its Own Span* into print in both English and German.

Molly Beswick knew Susan Bach for over four decades and was very familiar with her writing. It was therefore an especial help to me that Molly proof-read the book, particularly the chapters by Bach. Of course, remaining errors are my responsibility! Her heartfelt support for the project has been very sustaining.

The pictures described in chapter nine by Dr. Joy Schaverien were first published in *The Revealing Image* in 1991 and are reproduced here with the kind permission of the publishers, Routledge.

We are very happy to acknowledge *Psychosomatische Medizin*, Switzerland, for permission to reproduce Dr. Kaspar Kiepenheuer's work in chapter two, *Spontaneous Drawings of a Leukaemic Child.*

The Editor and Barbara Harborne are very grateful to the *Musée Picasso* in Paris for their great courtesy and helpfulness in enabling us to view the engravings we describe in chapter seven. We are also grateful to Mme. B. Baer, Paris, for giving us some time for a stimulating conversation. We should emphasise that the views expressed here are ours, unless specifically attributed.

Most of all I would like to thank all the contributors for their pieces, their close co-operation with me, and encouragement of the book as a whole.

Ralph Goldstein

Notes on the Authors

Paul Brutsche, Dr. phil., born 1943 in Basel, Switzerland. Since 1975 working in private practice in Zürich, Training analyst and lecturer at the G.G. Jung-Institute. For several years has been Director of the Picture Archives at the C.G. Jung-Institute. Past President of the Swiss Society for Analytical Psychology (SGfAP) and Past President of the C.G. Jung-Institute, Zürich. Presently member of the Curatorium and President of the Susan Bach Foundation. Writes articles and lectures in Switzerland and abroad, mainly on the themes of Picture interpretation, Art and Creativity.

Bill Burritt was born in Brantford, Canada; except for two years in Western Canada, southern Ontario remained his base until moving to Massachusetts, USA, for post-graduate studies. It was here he encountered the work of Jung in greater depth; this encounter developed into his pursuing his analytic training at the C.G. Jung-Institute in Küsnacht-Zürich, Switzerland. Married with three adult children, Bill is in private practice in Cheltenham and Bristol, England. He is active in the Independent Group of Analytical Psychologists, a training program in London, as a member of the Preparation Committee. While cultivating his interest in the areas of mythology and analytical psychology, he also wants to ensure the time and space for some tennis, canoeing, and travel.

Michael Edwards studied Fine Art then trained and worked as an art therapist at the Withymead therapeutic community in Devon. He subsequently established and directed post-graduate Art Therapy training in Britain and Montreal, founding the first M.A. in Art Therapy in Canada. He trained as an Analytical Psychologist in Zürich, where he was also for some years Curator of the C.G. Jung Picture Archives, a large collection of paintings and drawings by Jung's patients. He is a former Chair of the British Association of Art Therapists, of which he is a Fellow and Honorary Life Member. He has contributed chapters to major books on Art Therapy and to various journals. He has broadcast on radio and TV in Britain and Canada and has lectured widely in Europe and North America. For some years he has been Director of the Champernowne Trust Annual Course in Analytical Psychology and the Arts at Cumberland Lodge, Windsor. Currently he works as an analyst and art therapist in Cornwall and London.

C. Toni Frey-Wehrlin, Ph.D., Professional member of the Society of Analytical Psychology and member of the Schweizerische Gesellschaft für Analytische Psychologie. Initiator and co-founder of the Clinic and Research Centre for Jungian Psychology (Zürichberg Clinic) in Zürich. Training Analyst of the C.G. Jung Institute, Zürich.

Ralph Goldstein, Ph.D., studied academic psychology and did research on hormonal influences in animal behaviour, funded by the UK Medical Research Council, and then took up a lecturing post at University College of Worcester. But the motivation for all this study was really to do clinical work, and, having a family connection with Susan Bach, began to study with her, particularly helping with *Life Paints Its Own Span*. He now does Jungian psychotherapy both privately and in the National Health Service and conducts research with spontaneous pictures in severe illness (AIDS / HIV) funded by the Omega Foundation, London. He is an Associate Fellow of the British Psychological Society.

Barbara Harborne studied at Homerton College and Newnham College, Cambridge, including art history under Michael Jaffe. She is currently Headteacher of a Manchester inner-city primary school. She has interests both as a practising amateur painter and as an avid gallery visitor. Her school was praised in its most recent Ofsted report for excellent relationships and particularly good provision for art teaching. She has two daughters, one completing A-levels and the other studying French with Philosophy at Sheffield university.

Kaspar Kiepenheuer was born in 1942 in Göttingen, Germany. He spent two years in public schools in the USA, and in Rudolf Steiner School and humanistic gymnasium in Germany. He undertook Medical studies in Berlin and Zürich and specialised in Paediatrics, followed by psychiatric and Jungian training in Zürich and London. He studied intensively with Susan Bach in Zürich at the Childrens Hospital, and in London. He also studied Sandplay therapy with Dora Kalff, Zollikon. He is a lecturer and control analyst at the C.G. Jung-Institute Küsnacht. He is a founding member of the International Association for Sandplay Therapy (founder Dora Kalff). Today mainly private practice for psychiatry/psychotherapy with children, adolescents and adults. His wife is a potter and sculptor, and they have three children (17, 13 and 1 year) and a big white dog.

Helene Shulman Lorenz has a Ph.D. in Philosophy and a Diploma from the C.G. Jung Institute in Zürich. She is the author of *Living at the Edge of Chaos: Complex Systems in Culture and Psyche* published by Daimon Press in 1997. While maintaining a private practice as a Jungian analyst, she has taught philosophy, psychology, and cultural studies at several universities in the U.S. She has been active in community and human rights organizations, has worked on several film, concert, and theatre productions, and has raised a family. Currently, she is Academic Dean and Core Faculty Member at Pacifica Graduate Institute in California.

Cedrus Monte, Ph.D., is a Diplomate of the C.G. Jung-Institute, Zürich where she lived and worked from 1987 to 1998. Originally from California, she now resides in New Mexico. In

11

addition to pursuing classical Jungian studies, her central concern has been the exploration of the interface between spirit and matter, particularly as experienced through image-making, the psychodynamics of the body, and cross-cultural spiritual disciplines, including Tibetan Buddhism and Native American traditions.

Joy Schaverien, Ph.D., is a Jungian analyst and art psychotherapist in private practice in Leicestershire. Trained initially at the Slade as a painter, she has worked as an art therapist in the National Health Service, in a therapeutic community, adult psychiatry and out-patient psychotherapy. She was course leader of the Master's programme in art therapy at the University of Hertfordshire and now lectures widely in Britain and abroad on the links between art and psychotherapy. Among her many publications are *The Revealing Image: Analytical Art Psychotherapy in Theory and Practice* (Routledge, 1991) and *Desire and the Female Therapist: Engendered Gazes in Psychotherapy and Art Therapy* (Routledge, 1995). She is an Associate Professional Member of the Society of Analytical Psychology in London.

Preface

This book is intended as a celebration of the dedicated and inspiring work of Susan Bach in the realm of spontaneous pictures, which was published in comprehensive form in 1990 as *Life Paints Its Own Span: On the Significance of Spontaneous Pictures by Severely Ill Children* (Daimon Verlag). My wider claim is that, taken together, the chapters in this volume represent a Jungian approach to some fundamental questions about the quest for inner order in human experience.

Albert Camus described science as "man's attempt to satisfy the wild longing for clarity whose call echoes in the human heart". Analytical Psychology's response to this call has been to listen to the manifestations of images and symbols and to trace their heritage. This is the world of the numinous, of religious order, of archetypes and synchronicity. These distinctively Jungian interests are all to be found in Susan Bach's work and life and are represented in the work of the contributing writers. In paying tribute to her life, this volume shows how fruitful Susan Bach's work has been and in turn links a unique line of research in pictures into the wider stream of Jungian thinking.

This book presents work by writers living in Switzerland, the United States and England. It is a genuinely international collaboration as can be seen from the notes on the authors. There are papers by old friends and colleagues and others by psychologists who never met Susan Bach, but have read her work whilst making their own contributions to analytical psychology. Some authors have been assisted by one of the Susan Bach Foundations in pursuing their own research. It was my aim, as editor, to see if I could provide a strong taste of Susan Bach's own range of work, as well as the range of subjects in which she was particularly interested. Indeed, one of the most remarkable aspects of Susan's personality was her continuing interest in almost everything until the end of her life. Usually, she had a fresh point of view to add, or a surprising question.

Of course, the main interest of her working life outside the psychotherapeutic space ("the blue room") was in spontaneous pictures, and she pursued this work for fully 50 years. While the number of publications she generated was small by modern standards, the profound depths which she uncovered in her work make each publication a speck of gold. However, her major publications, *Spontaneous Paintings of Severely Ill Patients*, Geigy (8, Monograph, 1969) and *Life Paints Its Own Span* (1990) constitute a treasury of gold! Her book presents her findings and her method as they developed over the 50-year span of her work, beginning in a school in Germany (see the Preface of *Life Paints Its Own Span*).

The present volume opens with the last paper Susan Bach drafted before her final illness. It is worth printing for the depth of insight she developed into the nature and uses of spontaneous pictures. This chapter amply demonstrates how fundamental research into human nature need not be separated from clinical practice.

Dr. Kaspar Kiepenheuer worked very closely with Susan Bach on *Project White Child*. This project was the application of Susan Bach's method, worked out at the Neurological Hospital, Zürich with such co-workers as Hans-Peter Weber, Clinical Artist, to children suffering from leukaemia. In chapter 2, Dr. Kiepenheuer presents a profound study of one child, suffering from leukaemia, and his family. Once more, research with spontaneous pictures provides a deep insight into the progress of the illness and the sufferer's state of mind and "inner knowingness" about the prognosis. But such work also provides a meaningful bridge to the family and in particular to the siblings of the dying child.

Any psychologist, psychiatrist or psychoanalyst who is genuinely interested in the theories of C.G. Jung could not fail to be concerned with questions related to synchronicity and the difficulties of conceptualising acausal connections between biophysical objects. Similarly, philosophical questions arise from Susan Bach's original finding in 1947 that spontaneous pictures can also reflect the organic side of a person's total state (see, for example, Seligman in *Psychosomatische Medizin* **9**, 111-119, 1980) and from the discovery of "inner knowingness".

In chapter 3, Dr. Helene Shulman Lorenz considers the issue of "inner knowingness" – the profound relationship between psyche and soma – by extending Gregory Bateson's developmental sequence of cultural and personal learning to the transcendent function. At this level of development, balanced on the margin, there is an openness to synchronicity.

In chapter 4, Dr. Kiepenheuer, beginning from spontaneous pictures, approaches the synchronistic elements operating in psychosomatic illness. Dr. C.T. Frey-Wehrlin gives us some profound insights in chapter 5 from his own clinical experience, demonstrating the nature of synchronistic events, and the difficulties posed for conventional thinking by the need to engage with such phenomena. Dr. Frey-Wehrlin has been a long-time colleague and friend of Susan Bach, and so it is especially appropriate that he has written a chapter in her memory.

The opportunity first to become conscious that something synchronistic in nature is happening and then to place it into some personal context depends on the development of one's own story or journey (and this is also important in Lorenz' chapter). This problem is addressed directly by Bill Burritt in chapter 6, in which he illustrates the unique aspects of a Jungian standpoint on the relationship of the individual's story to the collective myth.

One of Susan Bach's interests was in the wider application of her method as worked out in detail in *Life Paints Its Own Span*. In particular, she considered the possibility of evaluating problems in Art History. Ralph Goldstein and Barbara Harborne pursue this hypothesis in chapter 7 by examining Picasso's well-known Minotaur series of engravings. The additional Jungian concepts of Animus and Anima were indispensable to this analysis, providing a link between Image and Meaning.

The longing for order is never stronger than in practical or therapeutic working with images. Dr. Cedrus Monte provides us with a fascinating insight in chapter 8 into how synchronistic phenomena may, so to speak, be invited by those willing and able to engage wholeheartedly in externalising their own experiences.

In chapter 9, we continue the movement towards the clinical setting. Dr. Joy Schaverien, who has done pioneering work in explicitly developing Art Therapy into Analytical Art Psychotherapy, integrates working with pictures into a wider theoretical understanding of transference and counter-transference. The pictures made by the artist-patient become part of the transferential network in a containing and safe way, both despite, and because of, the presence of desire.

Staying in the consulting room, Dr. Paul Brutsche, working in Switzerland, examines the vexed question of how a symbol can retain its healing capacity. In chapter 10, he writes movingly and clearly about therapeutic experiences using dreams. We learn how the meaning latent in a symbol, or an image, can constellate healing.

In chapter 11 Michael Edwards addresses the thorny issue of how pictures may appear to portray "inner knowingness" on some occasions, but not others. The essence of the problem is the question of generalisation of symbol, colour and composition from one occasion to another. Michael Edwards approaches these questions as they arise in Susan Bach's work and proposes the outlines of an answer in the theory of archetypes.

The final word is left to Susan Bach in her chapter on the question of humanising the properties of God, in order to relieve suffering. This topic has been the subject of lectures at the Jung-Institute in Zürich, by Dr. M. Odermatt (e.g. 1991), but Susan Bach was lecturing on this problem as early as 1956. The fundamental issue here concerns the displacing of the imagined properties of God onto individual human-beings; thus we end this memorial volume with an eternal question of image, meaning and myth.

Future Research and its Funding

The way forward has been sign-posted by Susan Bach in her setting up of the Omega Foundation (London) and Susan Bach Foundation (Zürich), both established towards the end of her life. These trusts were designed to provide assistance to scholars following interests related to her own (for which she herself never received any formal funding). This is not research for its own sake, but research in the service of providing therapeutic benefit. Susan Bach was a "scientist-practitioner" well before the term was coined.

The Objects of the **Omega Foundation** are as follows:

Assist research into new methods of alleviating the suffering of emotionally disturbed or seriously ill patients and / or those who may be facing death.

Help enhance the skills of physicians and other health professionals to assist patients suffering from a severe illness including suicidal tendencies, to discover their own inner resources and / or come to terms with their illness.

Help support specialised training of health professionals into ways of assisting severely ill patients and their families.

Help disseminate the results of such research by means of group discussion or conferences.

Correspondence concerning the Omega Foundation should be sent to the Chairman, Dr. Christopher Donovan, 25 Middleway, London NW11 6SH.

The Susan Bach Foundation, Zürich, is dedicated to supporting research into the relationship between Psyche and Soma. The areas of research relevant to this aim include among others: the constellating factor, synchronicity, hope as a life-giving factor, and spirit or numina expressing the ordering principle.

Correspondence concerning the Susan Bach Foundation should be sent to: The Susan Bach Foundation, c/o C.G. Jung Institute, Hornweg 28, CH-8700 Küsnacht, Switzerland.

A few Memories of Susan Bach

Since this book is a memorial volume, I have sought contributions from former friends and colleagues. Molly Beswick knew Susan Bach since the 1940s in England and was therefore in a very good position to remind us of Susan Bach's personal biography. Professor Hitzig knew Susan Bach professionally before, together with Verena Hitzig, becoming firm friends of Susan Bach's. Together they have written a memoir which gives us an insight into the professional biography. Kaspar Kiepenheuer provides a moving account of how Susan Bach could inspire growth both in the personal and professional spheres.

by Molly Beswick

Susan Ruth Bach, née Fleischhacker, was born in 1902 in Berlin, the second child and only daughter of a Jewish doctor and his wife.

One of her earliest recollections was of how the sewing woman who came to the house had made her a pretty apron with a matching lace-edged hankie and how, after an anxious search, she, Susan, was discovered sitting on the curbside, using the dainty handkerchief to dry the tears of a dirty little crying stranger. This impulse to help those in distress remained throughout her life.

As a small child she was regarded as a slow learner and was constantly in trouble for smelling everything about her, until it was discovered that she was severely short-sighted. With corrective glasses she learned fast and eagerly, particularly in the sciences, maths, literature and philosophy. Although she played no instrument, music was an early love. Bruno Walter as conductor, young Menuhin as performer, and Mozart as composer, particularly moved her heart, and when in old age deafness troubled her, she was still able to hear her favourite works with the inner ear.

She was also a passionate horse-rider and never forgot the advice of her instructors – "to sit correctly in the saddle, imagine an invisible thread which connects you to the zenith of the sky". This feeling of connection characterised the stance of her whole life.

At thirteen, when her mother was desperate with anxiety over her soldier son, Susan took over the whole running of the household, learning much which stood her in good stead in later life, including an ability to shop frugally and cook appetisingly.

Later, like her brother, she began to train for medicine, and this was abandoned only when it was discovered that she used her lunch-packs to bribe a fellow student to do the dissections she could not bear to carry out. Her studies were then transferred to mineralogy, again in a family tradition. She specialised in crystallography, learning gold and silver smithing so that she could create jewellery which would allow the stones to speak unhindered. It was a medal for outstanding research in crystallography which dropped through the letter box on the day she was forced to flee Berlin for England, unable to take the final examination for her doctorate.

Her Jewish studies had led her to a particular interest in the basic ideas of Hassidism, about which Martin Buber wrote. As a student attending one of his lectures she had asked him if he thought he was God's secretary to be so certain of what God said! But later he became a good friend.

It was an article she wrote for *Der Morgen*, the distinguished monthly periodical, which first introduced her to its co-editor, Hans Israel Bach, later to be her husband. Originally trained to be a concert pianist and later dismissed from his administrative post at the Ministry of the Interior by the Nazis, Hans Bach was a pupil and life-long friend of Leo Baeck.

Susan had, by now, been in therapy with a Jungian, Helene Wünsche, known as Wü, then running a home and school for disturbed children, to whom Hans and Susan turned on Kristallnacht. Wü warned them that she had had to hang a Nazi flag outside as protection, but without a second thought, offered them shelter and hiding. Susan remembered walking there with only a small suitcase through moonlit streets, where broken glass crunched underfoot.

She also remembered making a slice of opal in its matrix into a fob for a prominent Jewish friend, so that he could have something precious but unnoticeable – the matrix looked like leather – on him when questioned by the Gestapo.

By May 1939, it became too dangerous to remain in Germany and Susan and Hans fled to England, originally intending to then make their way to the USA, but finally deciding to stay so that the additional funds could be used for another escape from Germany. Arrived in England, they first worked as housekeeper and handyman in a Quaker home. Susan recalled attending the Home Office to be finger-printed – to her a proud mark of her uniqueness. Hans was later interned in the Isle of Man and by night she worked hard to reproduce his anti-Nazi book as an aid to his release. By day she used her analytic skills in work for the Association of Jewish Refugees.

On Hans' release they were lent a house and furniture by friends and took in a refugee boy, Ernst Hochland, who as an adult became the co-founder of the Manchester University Bookshop.

Another friend, Basil Anderson, of the London Chamber of Commerce's Hatton Gardens laboratory for precious stones, aided her application to study and work there on the search for cheap industrial diamonds, and encouraged her in the early development of micro-photography of precious stones. Susan retained her interest in stones throughout her life and until a late-in-life burglary, the house contained many beautiful specimens, in particular pieces of agate which she believed reflected the link between the plant and inanimate worlds, part of her belief in the link between all things.

It was her analytic work for refugees which took Susan Bach in 1941 to St. Bernard's Hospital where her interest in patients' pictures developed. For three years she conducted a study group on pictures to which ten mental hospitals contributed, studying the reflection of specific mental illnesses and evaluating the prognostic possibilities. In 1947 she first saw the organic aspects of such a picture. Later she lectured on the discovery to the Jung Institute, Zürich, and read a paper at the Burghölzli Clinic. From this arose the opportunity for years of research at the University Hospital, Zürich, the Neurosurgical Department, and later at the University Paediatric Hospital, Zürich.

A close friend of both Susan's and Hans', Culver Barker, sometime chair of the Analytical Psychology Club and founder member of the Society of Analytical Psychology, took a supportive and active part in her early research projects. A continuing interest in her work was shown by yet another old friend, Laurens van der Post.

While devoted to her research, she maintained her private analytic practice, always reserving time for those who could not afford the full professional fee, and using her skills and insights to help all those in her daily circle.

by Walter Hitzig

Susan Bach's special relationship with Zürich started in the thirties when she came to work with C. G. Jung who was then already a famous psychologist. This encounter was decisive for her future. She also worked with Toni Wolff.

In the 1940s in England Susan worked as a therapist in psychiatric institutions. In art work of her clients she discovered signs of deep-rooted or even life-threatening conflicts.

After the war she returned to Zürich for visits. She presented her ideas to C. G. Jung who encouraged her to continue collecting material. After a presentation in the psychiatric University hospital, the "Burghölzli", C. A. Meier, then professor at the Swiss Institute of Technology (ETH) as successor to C. G. Jung and director of the Jung-Institute, was also equally positive. Most important, however, it seems to me was the great interest exhibited by Hugo Krayenbühl, then chief neurosurgeon at our University: he offered Susan a collaboration with his service and gave orders to facilitate her work. Hans-Peter Weber, Dr. Krayenbühl's technical-scientific artist who had been appointed before the perfection of photography and TV to draw the results of operations, immediately became a real enthusiast of Susan's work.

He started to supervise and to help patients, mainly children, to draw, to paint, to model, briefly to express by figurative means their inner feelings. The result was one of the usual collection of pictures, as they accumulate in every children's hospital and even in every house with children. What was unusual, however, was the careful addition of an extract of the patients' disease history and the patients' comments at the time s/he was working on the picture. But most exceptional was the way Susan Bach looked at these products: for her nothing had been made by pure chance, but she always inquired for a connection with the life or disease of the patient. During these years, she became convinced that patients were able to accurately depict their somatic conditions. After several years of intensive work with Hugo Krayenbühl and Hans-Peter Weber in Neurosurgery, she decided to look out for a new field for her research.

Dr. Krayenbühl recommended her to me, because I was working at the Department of Paediatrics in charge of Oncology, caring for children with all kinds of tumours. I had always asked my little patients to draw me a picture, and I used to look at them with great pleasure, but without any ulterior motives. When Susan told me of her discovery of "body and mind drawings", I listened politely, but sceptically. Due to Dr. Krayenbühl's authority, I helped her to have access to children's drawings and to correlate them with the necessary data of their disease, but was busy with my other obligations.

My detached attitude changed dramatically after the first "seminars" of some of my group of haematologists with Susan Bach. Her method was very unusual and surprising for us, since she did not claim expert knowledge and explain the pictures to us as child psychiatrists usually did ("the tree has no roots, this means … the red colour means aggression …"). Instead, Susan was silent and pondered over the picture, looking again and again. Then she asked us: "what do you see?" In the beginning, sometimes a long silence followed which seemed even embarrassing, but she waited patiently. And then, hesitating answers came which we hardly dared to utter, because we thought they were too trivial or too far-fetched. Surprisingly, sometimes the youngest who in medical discussions never said a word would speak up and make surprising observations. Susan was always listening, encouraging, acclaiming and attentive. Many elements of the picture were built up in this way and the atmosphere became more and more animated. To conclude the session, again quite surprisingly, Susan would help the participants to summarize what they had seen and how they could correlate it with the actual disease. Thus, she practised a real sort of midwifery in the Socratic sense.

Within a short time, we were all convinced of recurring patterns in the pictures: children with leukaemia ("the white blood") hardly used any colors in the beginning; their persons, houses and landscapes were white or pale. Quite soon somebody (I think Susan) invented for our work the name "Project white child". I mention only one example, the second picture of such a boy, drawn a day after a blood transfusion. In striking contrast to the first white persons, it showed a well-fed man watering his garden with a red hose spreading red water over a green lawn, a moving demonstration of returning life and strength (see figure 6 in *Life Paints Its Own*

Span, Ed.). Many similar cases convinced us that really the physical state and the impact upon it of therapy could be expressed by the children in their drawings. The sessions with Susan soon became very popular in the hospital and were also attended by many interested staff members from outside the haematology department. In 1977 we organized a three-day workshop with several invited people which I baptized our "Bach-Festival". The main contributions were published in 1980 in *Psychosomatische Medizin (9,4)* (in English).

Hugo Krayenbühl and myself were so impressed by the originality of Susan Bach's idea concerning this ability of severely sick people to produce a pictorial expression of their somatic diseases that we proposed to the Medical Faculty to award her an honorary doctorate. Regrettably, in the judgement of the faculty's experts her approach was too subjective and could not be transmitted to others; in other words, she had failed to create her own "school". The proposal was therefore turned down. The experts' critique was to a certain degree justified, and we kept telling Susan afterwards that she must write down the essentials of her ideas in order to systematize them and to make them teachable. She was blessed by a long active life, and finally, in 1990, this book *Life Paints Its Own Span* was published and was immediately very well received. Had it been available in 1978, she might have earned the title of Dr. *honoris causa*.

Of course, I must mention here at least *pars pro toto*, her most important helpers: Dr. Hans Bach, until his death her faithful critical editor, Ernest Hochland, the experienced and knowledgeable man of letters and, last but not least, Robert Hinshaw who with never failing patience realized Susan's often extravagant wishes for her publications. She acknowledged all these (and many other) contributions with generous gratitude.

by Kaspar Kiepenheuer

When I met Susan Bach for the first time at the University Children's Hospital, Zürich, I was still almost a child myself, or at least that is how I felt as a budding paediatrician with little knowledge of what goes on inside a human being or, more importantly, inside a sick child. The experiences of watching children on their deathbeds got under our skins and was enough to render us speechless and perplexed. And then there was this little old lady from London who took us by the hand and together we studied the paintings and drawings of children looking for clues pointing to secret, hidden communications. Not only did I feel immensely consoled, but a new world opened up in front of me and it was under those circumstances that I found a completely new direction.

Fortunate circumstances and a generous clinic-director made it possible for me to spend nine months in London. I often stayed at the home of Susan and Hans Bach and soon felt very much a part of the family as if I had grown up there. Susan guided me through my work with childrens' drawings and paintings, helping me to unlock their deep and secret meanings. In her "Blue Room" I got my first taste of her work with the soul. At the same time my dreams began to express themselves in gushes turning into a rich source which to this day has not let up. When I left her home I felt like I was carrying my soul in my protective hands like a raw egg. Susan showed me how to respect the reality of my own soul as well as those of all the patients entrusted to me. This turned out to be such an overwhelming experience that my ego and the corresponding desire to be an important physician was pushed away into the background.

There is one other observation I made and that I will not easily forget; it was the way Susan and Hans Bach supported each other while performing their daily routines. I learned through those two human beings how to be thoughtful and considerate in dealing with the little things of everyday life, be it the preparation of a cup of tea or respect for the bluebells near the lovely holiday-cottage in Potters Bar. The small things grew into big things and my life became immensely richer through them and has been so ever since.

This collaboration with Susan was the guiding-light during my subsequent psychiatric and Jungian analytical training. Every experience I had was intensified through Susan's omnipresence, had a new meaning and made more sense. Not only am I grateful to her for helping me to develop a critical eye for comprehending the senses but also for giving me the courage to address the unknown and to make space inside myself for all that is still unrecognized. The Unknown – which is so magical – is paying me back in so many ways with a rich return during my daily psychiatric work. It was this "knowingness", or wisdom resulting from immersing myself in the drawings and paintings of sick children that henceforth guided my work and my personal life.

When writing her book, *Life Paints Its Own Span*, she came to Zürich quite often. I then had opportunities to be at her side and to help her deal with the sometimes apparently too complex daily life. I was grateful to be able to return some of the loving care that she had given to me so generously, now that she was feeling her age and was losing her strength. Yet this sensitive old lady still had moments when she could display incredible toughness, when – where it really counted – she would mercilessly pursue a straight line, true to her beliefs, even when occasionally this caused tempers to flare. She would be like a tyrant almost to a point where one would rather like to turn one's back on her. But there was always the sweet aftertaste because she was right and correct in making her point. Her book, once published in English and German, proved to me that her stubbornness was more than justified.

During the last months of her life she started work on a new project: "Children dream for their parents' sake". I feel sorry now that I met her frequent invitations to join the project with too much hesitation. I would have loved to soak up those last inspirations while being face to face with her. But as a small consolation I keep reminding myself that it was Susan who was the stimulus behind my ability to immerse myself in my work with such intensity.

Now that she is gone, her legacy remains. It is she who without any dogmatic and religious pretensions, but with the honesty of a child, pointed out to me through the drawings of children the comfort that can manifest itself. As a personal example, she said to me: "How the angels will be delighted that your father still bought a flute so soon before his death." Thus she presented to me a deeply felt faith and the fascinating phenomenon of synchronicity. Only a few days after her death my mother died, and saying "goodbye" to both my spiritual and my biological mothers did not cause any deep cuts, but quite to the contrary it opened up my horizon.

I am forever grateful, Susan.

1

Small Circles – Closed Early: On the Stories behind Dying Children's Pictures
A Contribution to their Evaluation

by Susan R. Bach

For decades we have studied spontaneous pictures,[1] especially those by children, because they are psychologically revealing. The recognition that the somatic side is also reflected in such paintings came to me in 1947[2] when I looked at the drawings of a chronically ill patient who was facing a leucotomy operation. The understanding of her paintings led to a revised diagnosis and treatment. Following up these insights, I found in many thousands of drawings that they reflect, apart from the psychospiritual situation, the patient's specific physical illness expressed in typical colours, shapes, numbers and motifs. These drawings can show the present acute states and point back to past traumatic events (accidents, birth of a sibling, death of a loved person). Often ahead of recognized symptoms, they may indicate the future development of an illness, even asymptomatic processes which, at the time, could not be diagnosed clinically. This methodical evaluation, developed and presented in my book, *Life Paints Its Own Span* (1990), revealed that a patient's picture language can reliably give significant clues to questions, which could not be answered on the basis of clinical data alone. The patient "tells us" himself through the non-verbal communication of his pictures.

The new insight I have arrived at is that we had not looked sufficiently at the outer concrete reality of the shapes and figures "chosen" and depicted. Originally, we were concentrating, for example, on the number of rungs in a ladder as relating to onset of illness, to the position of a tumour, to the child's age and the duration of his life-time. Here we include the boy's own

---

[1] This is the last paper written by Susan Bach and was completed by R. Goldstein. It was immediately preceded by *The Eye of Childhood: Children paint their parents' and families' situations* which was seen into publication in *Harvest* 1996, vol. 42, 1, by Dr. Frey-Wehrlin.

[2] See especially p. 104 and figure 40 of *Life Paints Its Own Span*, Bach, 1990

Figure 1.1 Peter, Policeman and Burglar

relation to a policeman in a more outward reality. This also makes us pay more attention to what the child said. The aim in mind now is to help the child to die in greater peace.

As an example we refer to Peter's picture, "Policeman and Burglar" (Figure 1.1). Peter was admitted to the Neurosurgical Clinic, Zürich, at 8 $^1/_4$ years suffering from a brain tumour and metastasis. The picture shows a policeman, as tall as the house, shooting blindly at a burning aeroplane. He is oblivious to the burglar who, perched between the tenth and eleventh rungs of the ladder, and in the boy's words "has climbed into the house. In his sack are the stolen goods." Had the child ever had an encounter with a policeman in real life? Or been threatened with punishment by a policeman when he had done wrong? Has he ever experienced a burglary? Were his treasures stolen and when?

What do we hope from reactivating the child's memory? Will it lead us back to the point at which his illness started? To the place which Culver Barker (1972) called his "original hurt" – possibly the place from which healing may come?

How will we find out? *By moving from picture language to verbal language.* Let him tell the story of the person he painted, of a broken tree, of a house on fire. Children love telling stories (and quite a few of us adults too). If he cannot start by himself, let us use the magic word "we" and "together" and ask the person in the picture, then write down what he says. Some children will be proud to dictate to us and find that we take seriously what they have to say, but others may stop talking altogether. At the same time it would strengthen the relationship between the patient and all his clinical carers. We have occasionally found some written comments, or words, or letters on their drawing sheet, which would give us an easy start to such a

Figure 1.2 Peter, St. Nicholas, Schmutzli and the Teddy Bear calling for help

conversation. At times their comments or remarks to Hans-Peter Weber, our much loved clinical artist at the Neurosurgical Hospital in Zürich, the doctor, the nurse, although recorded, were not used as I now suggest we might do.[1]

A verbal communication may be useful in the clinical situation in many ways. If the doctor, nurse or carer could *converse* with the patient and his drawing, it would greatly help to take the child out of his aloneness, give him the wonderful warm feeling of sharing. It would certainly give an additional task to the occupational therapist not only to work with the child in drawing a picture, but to go along with him to long-forgotten "sins" and, possibly equally important, remembered moments of happiness and fulfilment and link up with them for guidance in the use of their remaining life-time. Here notes of what the child has to say would help us towards a better comprehension of the total condition of the dying child. For instance, Peter commented that the "disobedient one is in the sack". Much as we are concerned with healing and treatment, for the dying child the question is what best use to make of his remaining life.

Our aim here is how to assist the child to live his small circle of life as creatively as possible, to die with a feeling of fulfilment rather than with feelings of guilt and fear. Hopefully, recovering children may have another chance and start on a spiral back into life.

Let us consider what can be practically attempted in this respect. For example, I remember a 14 year-old Italian boy suffering from leukaemia. His father had come to Zürich to stay the last few weeks of life with his only son and heir at the University Paediatric Hospital, Zürich. When visiting him with his father present and Professor Hitzig with us, I asked him for his

[1] See chapter 2, by Hans-Peter Weber, on collecting spontaneous pictures, in *Life Paints Its Own Span.*

wishes; he had three. He knew at once – one linked up with his father to take him for a ride through Zürich. The second wish was to visit the zoo and the third wish was to go for a swim. All were duly fulfilled. The reaction was impressive and his father could take him home to his native town. He lived for many months and died fulfilled, even leading some social life with some young girlfriends.

To this day I cannot quite fathom out what brought about the change, but since then I have introduced the "Three Wishes", for in this way the child can express what is latent in him, regarding his hopes for his remaining life-time.

Although I am aware that we cannot have a conversation with a child who died long ago, we will now illustrate what such a conversation might have been by using two sets of drawings. Rare as words or letters are in children's pictures, they enable us to use them as a starting point for a possible conversation, dialogue or even "trilogue", if one includes the picture.[1]

We will look first at one coloured picture and its carbon copy drawn by Peter whom we have met in connection with the picture "Policeman and Burglar". In this drawing (Figure 1.2), a colourful St. Nicholas walking to the left, is followed by his servant Schmutzli, earless and armless, with a little teddybear-like figure in his sack calling for help. "Help for what?" was our question.

Four days later (after making *this* picture) as the boy prepared to draw another picture (Figure 1.3), he asked for a sheet of carbon paper. Hans-Peter Weber, although not at all understanding why this should be wanted, brought him one. And so we have not only the picture of St. Nicholas, the patron saint of children, but both the colourful figure and, shall we say, the saint in his shadow aspect on the carbon copy.

One may be tempted to discard the carbon copy as, in fact, I had originally done. It was only when I studied the picture systematically much later, that I could see, with amazement, its possible significance.

Let us look at the difference between the coloured drawing and the carbon copy. In the top drawing the boy used all the colours at his disposal and commented: "The disobedient one is in the sack" and "All the good things are running out". In the carbon copy the colours are gone, but for the dark green with which the human figure in the sack is marked.

We note first that "all the good things" are now in the grey carbon copy. There are eleven of these; the boy died when eleven years old. Secondly, we note that he had added in green, the colour of life, four strange markings inside and six outside the sack, adding up to ten, his present age. And thirdly, the letter 'H', also in green, above the human figure, is added. What could it mean?

---

[1] The notion of such a "trilogue" is developed in the context of transference wishes in art psychotherapy by Dr. Schaverien in chapter 9 [Editor].

If we put the two pictures next to each other, how might we "translate" the differences? Has colour, but for some green, gone out of the life of this boy? Does the 'H' stand for "Help!" (German: *Hilfe*)? And, if so, is he calling for help against the power of the saint?

Comprehended in this way, the copy of St. Nicholas is not just a "copy" of Figure 1.2 to be discarded as not significant. Do we have here one of the many pictures which contain a heart-rending forecast of being carried away into the unknown?

What could we have done, how would we have responded had we understood the possible significance of St. Nicholas? Here he is no longer the patron saint of children, but rather a destructive, all-powerful shadow figure.

We might have felt that this child may well have experienced how something, or someone, good and utterly trustworthy had turned from being a friend into an enemy. The human figure in the sack had even called for help, for understanding and support. But to no avail, "nobody heard". Drawing the picture may have brought into his young mind an old experience of small "sins", never discovered and never explained. Does Peter experience illness as a punishment – as expressed in his words, "The disobedient one is in the sack"?

If I, or somebody else, could have understood these pictures in time, what might they then have taught us? We have the 'H' for help, so we may take on his call and set out together with Peter to hear what happened to Teddy Bear, to the small person helplessly carried away in the sack. If we could have shared the boy's fears and forebodings, then at least he might not have felt so alone and forlorn. In factual reality he died a most painful death.

Although we can no longer help Peter, what can we learn for other children experiencing similar moments of despair? We certainly need to express that we feel with them. For example, we could even consider having a word with St. Nicholas and explain to him how the disobedience came about. Although this would not change St. Nicholas in his determination, it may help Peter to understand better what happened. At best it may lead from understanding to forgiveness at last. In short, to humanise a child's comprehension of good and evil, of God and the Devil.

As our second example we have a comment by Marina, a little girl of 6 years and 10 months, suffering from leukaemia and treated at the University Paediatric Hospital, Zürich. Again we describe two pictures, which she drew during her treatment, together with her own comments.

Marina was a rather reserved child and when admitted to the hospital she would neither talk nor eat. She drew a picture showing a tilted red house with a brown roof (Figure 1.4). The house had no windows or doors, no earth, no sky, no sun. She commented later: "This is a cowshed – the cows are mooing because they are hungry. The farmer has gone into the woods and forgotten them. Nobody comes." So she felt utterly alone.

It was decided that someone *should* come and Dr. Agnes Herz from the Psychiatric Outpatients Department for Adolescents in Zürich was called in. She made good contact with the little girl. After two sessions there was already a marked improvement in the young patient, both physically and psychologically. Two months later she painted her last picture (Figure 1.5).

Figure 1.3 Peter, St. Nicholas and the Teddy Bear calling for help, carbon copy

Figure 1.4 Marina, Nobody comes

Figure 1.5 Marina, Manöggeli

The child said: "Manöggeli (a funny man, or manikin, in Switzerland) has eaten a lot and feels well. All the birds (seven, drawn in mauve) are flying to heaven, but the smallest one will get there first." On the ground seven 'Bergtrollblumen' are growing. "They are so lovely", said the little girl. The last on the left is without flower. We also note that the fingers on both hands, neither reflecting the natural number, add up to seven. Seven days later Marina died peacefully in her seventh year.

I hope that these two examples illustrate how our own reaction to what a child says is very different when we take their remarks as expressions of how they are feeling at that moment, rather than when we were concentrating on the research project concerning the psyche-soma relationship.

Finally, there is the reaction of the medical profession to be considered, unable to save the young life, that the child has hardly started to live. Undoubtedly, there is also the feeling of the parents that the much-wanted child, conceived and born at last, is now taken away so early. But there is still the opposite feeling contained in the words "Whom the gods love they call early". I am still puzzled how to bring the two together.

My personal hope is that apart from a new, fresh approach to the understanding of the spontaneous pictures of dying children, taking such pictures purposefully in their verbal aspect may reactivate and reach deeper layers, and lead us nearer to the world of the yet unknown, but potentially knowable, to the world of Inner Knowingness.

References

Bach, Susan R. (1990) *Life Paints Its Own Span: On the Significance of Paintings by Severely Ill Children.* Switzerland: Daimon Verlag.
Barker, Culver M. (1972) *Healing in Depth,* (Ed. H.I. Bach). London: Hodder and Stoughton.

2

Spontaneous Drawings of a Leukaemic Child: An Aid for More Comprehensive Care of Fatally Ill Children and Their Families

by Kaspar Kiepenheuer

This paper[1] is devoted to the case and life history of an individual child, Adrian, who suffered from acute lymphatic leukaemia from the sixth to the ninth year of his life. During this period he made more than 300 drawings, of which only a small selection can be examined in the space of this paper. I gratefully acknowledge the insights I gained into the inner experience of this very reserved child as a result of studying and evaluating some of the somatic and psychological contents of these pictures with Susan Bach. This offered me a strong supportive basis for communicating with him. And, finally, this form of communication helped to lead his parents and brothers out of their isolation and mute bewilderment.

Summary of the Medical Record

Adrian, born on April 1, 1965. The diagnosis of leukaemia was made when he was six years old. After an initial hospitalisation of six weeks, he had regular check-ups in our out-patient department. Meningeal involvement was found in March 1973. There was a bone marrow relapse and brain infiltration in October 1973. Meningeal involvement started again in February 1974, and bone marrow relapse in March 1974. In the intervals that were free from relapses and complications the child was in satisfactory general condition and was able to go to school. On June 26, 1974, a bone marrow transplant was performed after preparation of the patient with high doses of antileukaemic medication and whole-body radiation while he was

[1] This paper was first published in *Psychosomatische Medizin,* Heft 1/2, Band IX, 1980, S. 28-38. Reprinted with permission.

Figure 2.1 The Family (November 1971)

being cared for in a sterile unit. On July 12, 1974, the child died of a serious pulmonary infection.

All the titles of these pictures were given by the author.

Figure 2.1: Through this picture we are introduced to the family: to the left we see Adrian himself, with folded arms, head slightly inclined and his mouth strangely rectangular and stiff. However concerned and preoccupied we are with the fate of the patient, we do not want to forget that, in the background, there is a family affected and suffering in its own way. Thus, it is all the more helpful to have our attention drawn to the family situation by means of a picture like this. Children and parents are drawn in two separated frames. The two younger brothers are clearly removed from Adrian, the older one; they seem to be in the background; C. stands with raised arms and laughing; W., the smallest, is characterized as a cry-baby by his wide-open mouth with lines coming off from either side. Strangely, both parents have no arms! In connection with their facial expressions, that gives me the impression of helplessness and perplexity.

In a talk with the mother, we learned that little W. draws attention to himself not only by his crying, but also by continual bed-wetting, while his big brother – and perhaps rival – has, through his illness, become the centre of his parents' interest. C., on the other hand, was more and more often given the difficult task of standing in at home not only for the bigger brother, but even for the parents when they had to accompany Adrian to the hospital. Finally, he too had to see a doctor on account of his troubled sleep and stomach aches.

Figure 2.2 The White Nightmare (Summer 1973)

Figure 2.3 Between Heaven and Earth (In hospital, November 9, 1973)

Figure 2.2: Only rarely do we get the drawn representation of a dream from a child. Adrian pictures himself with a highly raised head. Above it there is a large expanse painted white like a carrier or frame of the dream contents. An unrecognizable figure in a muffled disguise enters, running. It is followed by a shape which the boy referred to as a ghost (additionally, it looks like a moving white blood cell with a black nucleus). Close by we see a symbol representing death, well-known to the boy. One cannot help wondering how Adrian will manage to face all these things and take them into himself, especially when one compares these three threatening symbols on the large white expanse with the small white head of the child himself. However, here in the picture he was able to convey these inner experiences impressively and colourfully.

From the case history, we learn that a leukaemic infiltration of the meninges had already started. Only a few months later the first bone marrow relapse occurred.

Figure 2.3: Under its large, red wavy roof, this house is remarkably low, as if cut off or sinking. Exactly above it is a pale red little figure: half-man half-bird, his arms (or wings) raised towards the threatening red weather in the West. The crown of the poorly rooted tree seems to be aflame, and a small black figure (perhaps a bird) is just about to raise his wings and take off.

Adrian has been in the hospital for four days on account of a bone marrow relapse and a leukaemic brain infiltration with a focal epileptic fit: this, a double acute process which may be reflected pictorially in the roof of the house and the crown of the tree. As a result of this, both house and tree seem to have become equally uninhabitable. Still, the anti-leukaemic and anti-epileptic therapy proved sufficiently effective, and in the picture "he" gets solid brown earth under his feet again. Less acute, but no less numinous is the impression created by the four black clouds and the four black birds. Exactly four months later, we were bewildered to discover there was a further relapse.

Figure 2.4: The title of the picture corresponds to that of the fairy tale from *1001 Nights* in which Ali Baba (the same initials as our patient!) gains secret admission to the cave of the robbers by the magic formula, "Open Sesame". Ali Baba skillfully evades the robbers' pursuit, and the tale ends with the outwitting and killing of all 40 robbers by Ali Baba and his cunning servant.

Let us concentrate first on the description of the picture: it is divided into two halves. To the left, halfway up, and "floating" like a mirage, the child draws the treasure cave. At a conspicuous distance from this, five figures take up the right half of the picture. In their midst is a kind of skeleton man, consisting of twelve white parts – a traditional way of presenting death. In his raised hand, he holds a saw (Ali Baba is a woodcutter, after all). Through his wide open left eye, he looks straight into the eye of the beholder and – the drawing child! This observation I owe to Susan Bach. Indeed, it proves helpful to relate the position of the drawing patient to each of the figurative representations. We take note of this "White Death" (leukaemia, leukos = white), and all the more so as he does not appear in the fairy tale. Three of the figures, presumably robbers, seem to be pointing grim looks and shiny weapons at him. Their attitudes are strangely ambivalent: for instance, the hand of one of them is timidly reaching backwards. The fourth manikin at the bottom of the picture goes his own way; his brisk pace, his weapon and his open look all point left, in the direction of the cave, and make him a great contrast to the others with their ambivalent attitudes. This fourth manikin is drawn in more vivid colours too. He passes just beneath the skeleton man's saw: his clothes are curiously "sawed" at the edges.

In evaluating the picture, we try to grasp the child's whole personality, i.e. to understand the picture as a representation of his physical and psychic condition. As a *physical* image, this picture may reflect the desperate struggle with the "white illness". The "burning" red light on one of the heads reminds us of the meningeal infiltration which was once more occurring at that time. The three black flashes of lightning on the other head look like a pictorial representation of the head radiation. It follows that the sharp weapons might be a compliment to our (passingly successful) therapy. And it is perhaps thanks to this that the manikin at the bottom of the picture "made it" once more; with renewed vigour and colour, yet marked by the saw of death, he can turn towards another goal – the cave with its promising treasures.

If the picture is evaluated *psychologically*, the two sides appear separated from each other by a long distance, a yawning void: on the one hand, there is a vigorous rebellion against illness and dying; on the other, something remote, promising, static and restful. This hiatus between the two realms could be understood as a call to accompany the child on his way and to help him build a bridge from one side to the other.

A short time later the child had a second bone marrow relapse which was again overcome by radical therapeutic measures. Adrian's decisive cooperation at that time impressed us.

Figure 2.5: On waves splashing high, the big-bellied ship sails from left to right. On deck there are ten Vikings of various sizes and colours, and with an assortment of weapons. All the weapons are raised: swords, lances, clubs, sabres and daggers. Strikingly, there are only nine shields at the disposal of ten Vikings! Six blood-red stripes cover a part of the bulging sail. On the white space after the sixth stripe would be room for about three more stripes. Above, in the masthead, is an eleventh Viking. He looks through his telescope in the direction they travel, to the right. In the usual style of this gifted child, the seven strokes above this Viking's head probably denote that something has suddenly caught his attention. The existence of this far-seeing man offered me a welcome opportunity to start a conversation with Adrian. It struck me again and again how important it was for this reserved child that I should take note of the contents of his drawing. He asked me to describe the picture down to the last detail. After I had duly admired it, its many colours, the weapons, etc., I asked: "And who is that up there?" Since there was no reply, I went on to ask: "What does he see in his telescope?"

He said: "Another ship."

Some weeks later I asked him again who was up there. He replied: "That's you!"

Figure 2.4 Ali Baba and the 40 Robbers (Winter 1973/1974)

Figure 2.5 The Viking Ship (for Mother's Day, May 12, 1974)

Figure 2.6 Three Wild Animals (drawn in hospital, May 14, 1974)

Figure 2.7 The Pirates and Their Ship (drawn in the sterile unit on June 26, 1974)

Once again, Adrian expressed himself by means of a far distant epoch, even one steeped in legends, the medieval Vikings, bold seafarers of the North. Alerted by Susan Bach, my attention was drawn to the significance of numbers in this picture, especially in relation to some biographical data: if the six blood-red stripes correspond to six healthy years of life, we can estimate how much room remains for the following "white" (leukaemic) years. If the ten Vikings have only nine protective shields, what happens to the tenth in the case of attack? Or, again in terms of the same time unit, what will happen in the tenth year after nine protected ones? The course of the illness provides a deeply moving answer.

Yet, from another level, so to speak, something new is in sight so significant that it is worth seven little strokes to the boy artist. That he links the doctor who takes care of him with this far- and fore-sighted figure may perhaps be taken as a confirmation that he felt inwardly understood in our kind of dialogue. That encouraged me to continue on the same level, pursuing at the same time, however, the haematological procedures.

Figure 2.6: In the lower half of a big sheet, Adrian drew "Three wild animals hunting something unknown", as he explained to his nurse. When studying this picture with Susan Bach, we were puzzled by the word "hunt" as we looked at the expressions of these animals. They seem to be bracing themselves against the direction in which the "unknown" is supposed to be. Their coats and even the ground they walk on are bristling. They bare their teeth, show their orange-pink tongues, and their stiff tails and ears express a mood of alarm. Adrian meant to rub out the small animal to the right with its faint pencil outlines. Instead, "by mistake" he took the yellow crayon: a yellow line cuts through the head and one paw of the animal.

In conversation with the child, the "unknown" did not become more evident. But the previous as well as the actual course of the illness provide sufficient cause for the gravest misgiving. Because of a renewed focal epileptic fit, Adrian is undergoing heavy anticonvulsive treatment. Further relapses and complications are certain to occur. Only a bone marrow transplant might still provide a chance of recovery, however slim.

In order to experience this child's view of his own physical and psychic state through this drawing, I tried to put myself into the situation of these animals, to slip into their skin as it were: the ground is shaking and trembling beneath one's feet; the feeling of fright and terror in the face of something gruesome is piercing. One would like to scream. The child's inner fears – so vividly illustrated in this picture – were perhaps all the stronger as they were not expressed verbally. From then onwards our medical team encouraged his parents to talk frankly to him. His father told him about the nature of his illness, about the serious prognosis, the importance of medication, etc. Thus, considering the chances and dangers of the planned bone-marrow transplantation, we could talk very openly with him.

With admirable courage, Adrian entered a sterile unit in preparation for this serious operation. What he felt during this phase, the following drawing may illustrate:

Figure 2.7: The picture was a present for the chief nurse of the department, whom he called "Sheriff" in jocular consideration of her rank. In the left corner of the picture, we see twelve pirates, as the child called them himself. Some are only half visible. They carry many kinds of weapons and appear in full attack. Some lack a leg, an arm or an eye. The fat, athletic pirate in the foreground is particularly conspicuous. He has three weapons: a dagger, a sabre with a strange (skull-like!) handle as well as a big pistol whose shot – in the middle of the picture – is aimed at the shadowy form on the right. According to the child, it is a ship belonging to the pirates. Its outline is barely recognisable. Of the two portholes, the one on the left seems to look like a proper eye; the other is empty (blind?), and a ladder with rungs leads inside. The twelve pirates are separated from their ship by a grey, rising kind of threshold.

With the external, *physical* interpretation, one could be tempted to see among the pirates not only our "Sheriff" chief nurse, but also all the other members of our team who fight against Adrian's leukaemia; or, the child himself in his physical fight and his co-operation with our antileukaemic measures. The weapons (our therapy?) are impressive. But are they effective? The child's pictorial language indicates a lack of co-operation and integration in this fight. Susan Bach, as she looked at this picture, was reminded of the disintegrated, pathological growth of leukaemic cells. The Sheriff's pistol dominates the picture. That very day an important and incisive injection had to be carried out after it had been explained to Adrian. The picture tells us how this "shot" may have dominated his feelings and thoughts! The whole body radiation, planned for a few days later and also discussed with the child, may be announcing itself and its "burning out" effect in this burnt-out ship.

Let us now look at the drawing as a representation of the child's *inner* experiences. Again, two opposed worlds are facing each other. To the left, colourful life, the daily courageous grappling with reality, but also unrest, confusion, contradictions. To the right, colourless, stiff, motionless and quiet: a death ship? As the picture tells us, the child seems to "know" that, however radical the operation, such a burnt-out shadowy structure cannot be saved anymore. On the contrary, it is already steering towards new horizons. Do the twelve rungs (for the twelve pirates?) not bear a gruesome resemblance to the ribs of the "death" in Figure 4 (twelve there, too)? Here they give access to the realm of the shadows. The visit to Hades was the twelfth and last of the labours of Herakles in Greek mythology, and surprisingly, Charon's boat that carried people across the river Acheron is depicted on Greek vases with an eye at the bow!

The threshold to this new horizon is low, the anchor is ready for weighing. Thus, the fight is still on.

Figure 2.8: Before he did this drawing, Adrian talked with his mother. Together, they thought of all the people who were praying for him. He drew with pencil on a green sheet of paper that he had chosen for himself. At the top is God with a halo, surrounded by clouds, fourteen stars and the crescent of the waning moon. Below are the names of his nearest and dearest who pray for him: Daddy and Mummy (in Spanish, his mother tongue); C. and W.,

Figure 2.8 A.'s last Picture (drawn in the sterile unit on July 4, 1974)

his brothers. The enclosed room below represents his sterile unit. He is lying stretched out on his bed. Above his head there "floats" what is presumably the content of his prayer: "healthy", plus an upright little figure with strong raised arms (cf. the bird-man in Figure 3), and next to it, a hand that seems to be pushing away four syringes. To the right, at a great distance from the child, there sits his mother, who had in real life – in sterile clothing – been able to participate to a considerable degree in the care of her child. She is also praying. Between them there is a table with a set of sterile instruments. Last, the child draws the seven beams between heaven and the sterile unit (see Bach, 1974/75).

Figure 2.9 Family Excursion to the Black Forest (C., 7 years old, August 15, 1974)

Figure 2.10 Greetings from Heaven (W., 5 years old, August 31, 1974)

This is the very last picture Adrian ever drew. How different it is from all the previous ones! There is no suggestion of fighting now. Peace has been made with the "other side", which is no longer unreachably distant (Figure 2.4). It is not something unknown and frightening outside the picture either (Figure 2.6), nor is it stiff and inanimate (Figure 2.7). No, in this picture the other realm proves to be the Kingdom of Heaven, peaceful and almost serene. In the context of the whole picture, I understand the word "Healthy [*gesund*]" in the child's prayer to mean redeemed, saved, hale (salvatus). After all, the small (soul) man with his raised arms points in the direction of God. The syringes that have been pushed aside suggest: Enough injections have been given; they are no longer necessary now. In contrast to previous pictures, here the void between the two facing sides is bridged by seven beams, although they do not actually reach the child's unit. Are they showing him the way? Having learnt to take seriously the significance of numbers in the drawings of our children, we ask ourselves what the number seven means for this child. Or, in the particular context of this picture and the child's situation: In what way do seven units separate this child from – or lead it to – Heaven?

To what extent this picture was right, only the further course of the illness showed. After the co-operative child had, at first, overcome the major operations, the medical record tells of the first feared side-effects. An obscure fever worried us more and more. We could not influence it with our medication. After seven days, on the night between the 11th and 12th of July, 1974, Adrian died of a serious lung infection. His parents were present, and told us that Adrian had remained fully conscious almost to the end and had died peacefully.

This picture is now kept by the parents as a legacy. Weeks after his death, we looked at it again together. In tears, Adrian's mother confessed to me: "Adrian has given us so much more than we could give him." Indeed, I too, had been deeply impressed by the inner composure and strength of this dying child. More and more his parents had become able, so to speak, to rely on his guidance. How much strength can be derived from deep religious convictions is shown not only by this last drawing, but also by a remark he made to his parents: "Jesus has given me so much strength that I shall get over anything that is coming now."

Afterwards – Back to the Living

On my regular visits to the family after Adrian's death, I wished to comfort the parents and to show them my sympathy. During these long evenings we faced many memories that emerged from the parents and Adrian's own drawings. We learned to see this child's short life as a life picture, a meaningful unity that had come full circle.[1] In spite of all their grief, the parents expressed a feeling of great happiness about this. On the other hand, one has to be

---

[1] Compare this feeling with Bach's chapter 1, *Small Circles – Closed Early* [Editor].

aware not to gild the memory of a child so much that he becomes an idol. Such a deviation from reality would again have condemned the two brothers to a forgotten, marginal existence. Their behaviour alarmed me already: the smaller, W., had stopped wetting his bed from one day to the next after Adrian's death, but promptly began again when I paid a visit to the family! C., on the other hand, was remarkably quiet and did not manage to utter one word concerning his dead brother. But when I turned to him and told him how pleased I would be to have a picture from him, he drew the following:

Figure 2.9: Onto a black sheet he drew, incomplete, the memory of a trip they had taken together to the Black Forest. When asked about the white fisherman, he said: "That is somebody." Urged further, he replied, very carefully: "That is Adrian." From then on, he was again able to pronounce the name of his brother.

W. expressed his relationship with his dead brother some weeks after Adrian's death as follows: "It is wonderful that Adrian is in Heaven with God. But now I want him to come back." His drawing shows us how alive the presence of his brother has remained for him.

Figure 2.10: According to the child's commentary, Adrian is above in Heaven near God waving down happily smiling. From below, he (W.), waves back, his look turned upwards. To the left, just on the edge as if looking round the corner, there are the parents and C. This is W.'s version, in continuation of Adrian's last picture, where all members of the family were also involved. It may be taken as his relationship between his world and the Beyond. W.'s fascination (or envy?) for his brother in Heaven became so overwhelming that he expressed his wish to die and join Adrian in Heaven, much to the parents' great terror. At their request, I then saw the child for psychotherapy.

The circle is complete when we turn back to the family picture (Figure 2.1), which had even then drawn our attention to some emotional needs of the individual members of the family. The tension and perplexity, which showed itself there, seems to have been resolved in Adrian's last drawing and C. and W.'s pictures.

All of us dealing with this dying child were not only deeply moved, but also fortified by the inner strength that he conveyed by his drawn communications. This helped us in our attitude toward his parents and brothers, and it also made us more sensitive in the psychological care we give to other dying children and their families. Above all, he helped us to see his fate (and in the end, our own!) – which was, after all, so bitter – in a new light. And this also allowed us to accept what happened instead of rebelling against it.

In our care of leukaemic patients and their families through illness and dying, our attention is drawn time and again to the urgent need that more be done. Clearly we see the need to bridge the gaps that exist in the care available for these children. I wish to stress the importance of such a bridging by a new term: "perithanatal" care (*Thanatos*, Greek = death).

Based on Adrian's drawings, I have tried to describe this task. In his case, it was possible for a bridge to be built from the child to the doctor and the nursing staff, from the child to his family, also from the physical to the psychological aspects of his illness, from the active struggle with the reality of illness to presentiments of the hereafter. And finally, our attention was bridged or drawn from the dying and dead child to those still living who were left behind.

Summary

The case history of a leukaemic boy (6 to 9 years old) is presented and illustrated by a selection of his spontaneous drawings. These were an invaluable help in the care of this child, i.e.:

- a criterion for his physical and psychic situation,

- an expression of his hopes and misgivings,

- a base for open communication with the child, and

- a bridge to the parents, who were thus enabled to experience the short life of their child as round and fulfilled.

After the boy's death intense attention was given to his two brothers, their feelings also being represented by their spontaneous drawings.

References

Bach, S.R. (1974/75), Spontaneous Pictures of Leukaemic Children as an Expression of the Total Personality, Mind and Body, *Acta Paedopsychiatrica*, **4**, 1, p. 100.

3

Wind-trails

by Helene Shulman Lorenz

You walking, your footprints are
the road, and nothing else;
there is no road, walker,
you make the road by walking.
By walking you make the road,
and when you look backward,
you see the path that you
never will step on again.
Walker, there is no road,
only wind-trails in the sea.

From *Proverbs and Tiny Songs*
by Antonia Machado (1995)

Susan Bach was lecturing at the C.G. Jung-Institute in Zürich the first afternoon I went there. She was eighty-three at the time, but had a strong voice and impressive presence commenting on slides of paintings by cancer patients she had collected at the Kinderspital in Zürich. She had made a long journey of her own by then, out of Germany before World War II with her husband to England, and fifty years of work in England and Switzerland studying spontaneous paintings. I was on my way back to Europe from the United States, where my family had immigrated between the two world wars. I was searching for footprints, lost mythologies, alternative visions of the world.

There is a Buddhist meditation instruction which says: "Leave your birthplace." When you leave cultural worlds behind, whether voluntarily or through forced migrations, you become an expert on making roads by walking. Many contemporary writers have suggested that an epistemological advantage can come from border crossings. At the frontier between two worldviews, one learns a lot about cultural constructions, the influence of place, and creativity. Susan Bach had forged new ground with her work, but what she offered would take me years to understand. Nothing in my positivist American education, which strictly separated mind and body, had prepared me to see what she was looking at.

How could I understand, for example, the story of the ten year-old boy who painted the picture of the red sun between mountains on the cover of her book *Life Paints Its Own Span*? A day *before* the operation, he painted a red-yellow sunball between two green hills. (See the book-cover and figures 70 and 71 and pp. 109 and 182 of Bach, 1990). A brain tumour can occur in one of four possible positions in the optic chiasma. During surgery a "chestnut-sized, solid, yellow-red tumor" (p. 109) was removed from a location on the optic nerve parallel to the location of the sun in the spontaneous drawing. The boy recovered well.

Another similar story concerns a Zürich artist who also knew about Susan Bach's work at the hospital. One day in June he felt he should make "a drawing in red and blue" (reproduced as figure 226 and described on p. 183 in Bach, 1990), and show it to Susan Bach. He held it across his stomach and wondered if it meant something about cancer, although at the time he felt perfectly healthy. By November of the same year he began to feel ill, and a tumour was diagnosed in December. In March of the next year a carcinoma of the colon was removed just over the area where he had held the red part of his painting ten months earlier.

These and many other similar stories led Susan Bach to postulate an "inner knowingness", as if, when we look behind us in time at what we have dreamed, painted, said or done, we can see that we have left "footprints", a "road", "wind-trails on the sea", which we could learn to read. Clearly this concept is outside the paradigm of current Western "official" medical science, yet Bach's work led her to believe that such inner knowingness is a constant potential. "If there is such 'knowingness' manifest in the pictures of patients, as well as outside the hospital setting at critical moments in life, can we dare to accept that we ordinary people may also be included in an invisible aura of 'knowingness'? In any case, we might start to look for it." (Bach, 1990, p. 186)

Cross-cultural research and familiarity with Jungian psychology had led Bach to believe that the awareness of such possibilities was widespread in past eras and current non-Western cultures. "Inner knowingness has been lived with for untold centuries … ". Many cultures and individuals practise divination, prophetic possession trances, ceremonies which include spontaneous drawings, and healing connected with visualization of images. "To say 'they know intuitively' does not do justice to the way they conceive of such powers – in the language of the Bushmen, they hear the tappings inside themselves, and the Old Testament speaks of the 'still, small voice within'" (*ibid.*, p. 186).

For years after I first heard Susan Bach speak, I tried to digest this information, to assimilate it to what I already knew. Modern cultural anthropology speaks of "shock theory" (Thompson *et al*, 1990), the more and more common event of encountering foreign cultural values or experiences which cannot be interpreted through current ways of knowing. In the contemporary environment of globalization, this happens often, and a huge body of theory is developing on the subject of paradigm shifts and intercultural encounters. But rarely do these theories discuss how difficult such a process can be personally.

As I continued my Jungian training in Zürich, and later began seeing clients, frequent synchronicities and cases of "inner knowingness", became part of my daily work. I experienced them as numinous and uncanny, a sure sign that such events were at the outer margin of my comprehension. Often, I discussed the problem while hiking around the mountains outside Zürich with a friend who was also in training as an analyst. She would say to me again and again, "An amazing thing happened this week." I began to see that was part of the problem: we could not see our own experience with these events as normal. As long as we saw such experiences as "amazing" we were constructing them as outside conventional thought. We were reaching for a new paradigm and fighting against it with all our might. In this way we were collaborating with modern Western philosophy since the 17th century, which imagines the world separated into mind and matter, ghosts and machines, culture and nature, active and passive, colonizer and dominated. To accept this world view, one has to divide both the outer and one's inner world into light and shadow, acceptable and forbidden. In the same year both of us suffered intense, long illnesses which I am sure were partly caused by a war in our souls, a somatization of a seemingly insoluble psychic problem. C.G. Jung warns against this. "The archetype – let us never forget this – is a psychic organ present in all of us. A bad explanation means a correspondingly bad attitude to this organ which may be thus injured. But the ultimate sufferer is the bad interpreter himself" (Jung, 1959, p. 160). Our obligation, according to Jung, is to find contemporary narratives for psychological experiences, which like many other complexities, reassert themselves outside the current Western medical paradigm. We have to "dream the myth onward and give it a contemporary dress" (*ibid.*).

In Susan Bach's work, as well as that of C.G. Jung, psyche and soma – our phenomenological experiences of self and bodily life – are intimately inter-related. Two young patients with cancerous brain tumours reported on in *Life Paints Its Own Span*, Peter and Priska, seem to Susan Bach to represent opposing attitudes to psyche and soma, life and death, in their drawings. Nearing death, Peter seems to feel himself being dragged fearfully toward oblivion by St. Nicholas, a "punishing power" connected with "his rankling feeling of disobedience and unforgivable guilt". Priska, on the other hand, depicts St. Nicholas as a positive force, leading her with a golden crook as she steals tangerines from his sack. Her imagery is related to her attitude toward psyche and soma. "Can we venture to grasp that Priska who is so positively related to the Saint, can die contentedly?" (*ibid.*) Peter, we could say, is living through a narrative which has dissociated psyche and soma, while Priska has found a way to integrate them. Susan Bach remains optimistic about healing possibilities, even for those who suffer from dissociative complexes, if Western healing professions could create a new type of healer: "Here I believe lies a task to be rediscovered for the physician and the helping professions, to follow the rainmaker of old, become the shaman of our computerized clinical approach, and help the human person to die or live in a state of greater harmony, wholeness, and peace." (*ibid.*, p. 189).

Very much is at stake when we are confronted with information which falls outside or at the edge of the consistencies with which we habitually interpret our environments. Shamans are generally "wounded healers", people who have had experiences outside the dominant paradigms of their culture, either through somatic illness or exceptional psychological events. Their own journeys of fall and recovery are often taken as evidence of their suitability to perform healing rituals, as if healing itself had something to do with border crossings. After certain kinds of crisis, there is a change of worldview: " … when you look backward, you see the path you will never step on again."

The American philosopher Gregory Bateson, who was himself a veteran of many travels and was later to die of cancer, called the habitual or conventional shared framework of cultural assumptions which any individual might have developed, "Learning II". He thought that as children, our explorations and insights might be more like trial and error, which he named "Learning I". Eventually we discover (and help to create through intersubjective dialogues) regularities in everyday experience which allow us to make routine more general, characteristic behaviors. If the environment changes, we can change routines without reflecting on the process. In fact, our environment and routines are constantly evolving in a kind of gradual unconscious intersubjective drift we interpret as regularity.

Bateson imagined that under certain circumstances, we might be pushed to a new level, "Learning III". Chief among these circumstances might be encountering paradoxes, "double-binds", insoluble problems, that no amount of habitual routine will sort out. He quoted a Zen master who said, "To become accustomed to anything is a terrible thing." Learning III provides feedback, and reshapes our schemata of psyche and soma in terms of situated learning. We discover that knowledge frames are contextualized by social location, rather than being universal.

Unfortunately, it is usually our characteristic behaviours and routines which allow us to create self-images. We become accustomed to ourselves and others as we have known them in specific cultural learning environments, and it is truly a terrible shock when painful somatic or psychological experiences shatter our habitual thought-patterns. Then we must imagine a world where there are multiple locations, from which knowing and imagining create interactive networks of parallel alternative worlds, even within our own psyches. To imagine identities as "wind-trails on the sea" is an enormous change of consciousness.

Bateson understood the paradigm shift in Learning III as extremely disruptive:

But any freedom from the bondage of habit must also denote a profound redefinition of the self. If I stop at the level of Learning II, 'I' am the aggregate of those characteristics which I call my 'character'. 'I' am my habits of acting in context and shaping and perceiving the contexts in which I act. Selfhood is a product or aggregate of Learning II. To the degree that a man achieves learning III, and learns to perceive and act in the context of contexts, his 'self' will take on a sort of irrelevance. (Bateson, 1972 p. 306)

Can we imagine that Priska, led by St. Nicholas with a golden staff, and Susan Bach herself, as well as the new generation of compassionate healers she hoped for, could experience Learning III?

Bateson believed we need to look for concrete examples to illustrate his ideas about hierarchies of learning, and that "art is commonly concerned with learning of this sort". Here he is developing a notion parallel to that of Jung's "active imagination" as a way to bridge conscious and unconscious symbolic structures. Bateson suggests that Learning III represents a difficult journey with a possible rewarding outcome:

For others, more creative, the resolution of contraries reveals a world in which personal identity merges into all the processes of relationship in some vast ecology or aesthetics of cosmic interaction. That any of these can survive seems almost miraculous, but some are perhaps saved from being swept away on oceanic feeling by their ability to focus on the minutiae of life. Every detail of the universe is seen as proposing a view of the whole. These are the people for whom Blake wrote the famous advice in *Augeries of Innocence*:

> To see the World in a Grain of Sand,
> And a Heaven in a Wild Flower,
> Hold Infinity in the palm of your hand,
> And Eternity in an hour. (*ibid.*, p. 306)

From a less lyric perspective, Learning III can be seen to have a relativizing effect on every embodiment of Learning II. According to Bateson, "The question is explosive." Learning III can generate "a network of contingencies which goes out in hundreds of directions … ". We might consider modern science a highly elaborated form of Learning II, that is as a local, socially-constructed method of learning to learn. Positivism, empiricism, Cartesian dualism, and laboratory techniques all represent conventions, or habits of thought, which artificially restrict the field of inquiry and thereby limit the variables to be recorded. What if they were only one way to approach knowledge and we had to imagine multiple, negotiated, dialogic possibilities depending on culture, goals, and social location? In 1972, when Bateson published *Steps to an Ecology of Mind*, many intellectuals in the West had not yet considered such a possibility. Today there is an intense debate about the subject in virtually every discipline. For some, the new paradigm evolving is experienced as an Armageddon of relativism. In the seventy-fifth anniversary issue of the *International Journal of Psychoanalysis*, editor David Tuckett wrote that without clear standards, psychoanalysis would degenerate into a "Tower of Babel":

Psychoanalysis today, to judge by what we know of both theory and practice, is in a state of considerable ferment. We have schools of analysis which appear to be entirely at odds with one another. We have extreme forms of relativism … (in Gillett, 1998, p. 137)

Commenting on this state of affairs after the publication of the "Anniversary Edition", psychoanalyst James Phillips (1998) had a different reading: "My reading was that the preponderance of authors espoused the conclusion that there are no theory-free facts in psychoanalysis … ". In fact, Phillips thought that the Anniversary Edition "might be considered the official announcement of the death of positivism in psychoanalysis".

This fear about loss of certainty has been called "Cartesian anxiety" (Bernstein p. 57, Commentaries) and could be understood in Bateson's terms as part of a transition to another level of learning. In fact, many disciplines in the contemporary Western academic world may be in a crisis of Learning III as a result of profound culture clash and critical theorizing. Western conventions of dividing the world into ontological contradictories like mind and matter, culture and nature, masculine and feminine, civilization and primitivity developed during the colonial and early modern eras. In the elite educational worlds of the time, white anthropologists and historians could write appalling racist commentaries on African or Asian cultures, and male psychologists and literary critics could create patronizing and infantilizing accounts of female motivations that went unchallenged, because they could be reasonably sure that their articles would be read by few of those they described. When university systems in Europe and America began to open to large numbers of women and people of colour, the whole issue of the social construction of disciplinary canons came intensely to the fore. A new literature developed, questioning the hidden scripts of domination in discourse. When nature (and femininity, colonial territory, tribal ritual, and popular culture) were characterized as primitive, innocent, "virgin", inferior, or passive, then control and exploitation could be seen as "civilizing" reform. Much post-colonial cultural theory is a rescue operation for counter-knowledges and counter-narratives that were put aside in hierarchical, colonial encounters. This theory requires Learning III.

The work of both C.G. Jung and Susan Bach can be seen as part of a globalized cultural transition toward the possibilities of Learning III. Jung was highly critical of the scientific paradigm of his time as applied to the psyche. He wrote:

Seen in this light, analytical psychology is a reaction against the exaggerated rationalization of consciousness which, seeking to control nature, isolates itself from her and so robs man of his own natural history …. People live as though walking in shoes that are too small for them. (Jung, 1969, p. 130)

It is not the case that fixed ontological entities, "the psyche" or "the mind" are separated from "the soma" or "the body"; it is the Western scientific construction of these concepts which has imagined them as dissociated. An alternative construction would imagine a continuous self-organizing activity in an active communal network full of paradoxical experience: a lived world, a self-regulating system with multiple distributed "intelligences", an autopoietic organism with non-linear dynamics, an embodied spirit with multiple possibilities for creative expression, situated histories, hermeneutic knowledge, dialogical rationality, narrative truths. What "heals" is what reconciles, that is, what provisionally allows for the broadest, integrated perspective on a complex, evolving environment. Any knowledge articulated by an observer in a self-organizing system feeds back into the whole, which is involved in the constant transformative processes of living systems. When the system gets rigid it dies. Rebirth and transformation are critical to life. Post-modern "cultural alchemy" is a worldview developing in a whole range of theories currently in play. In this view, whatever has been marginalized, forgotten, left behind, or split off, including alternative healing systems, can be examined as "footprints" for evidence about self-organizing systems at work.

In Susan Bach's long-term study of the paintings of critically ill children, we are provided with new ways to think about the relation of soma to psyche. In the presentation of this material, we are forced to think about fissures and erasures in the modern medical model, and to see our own inherited discourse, and perhaps our own psyches, as a patient suffering from "an estrangement of the soul from the body". In this reading, Susan Bach becomes one of the shamans she describes in her book:

> Long and specialized training and personal experience enable him to go relatively safely in search of the fugitive soul of the patient, and if possible, bring it back to the suffering body. He achieves this by performing a special dance which leads to a state of trance, of ecstasy. His aim is to bring about a reunification of psyche and soma: healing. (Bach, 1990, p. 82)

In her life, Susan Bach learned to trust her own "inner knowingness" through patient observation and interpretation of spontaneous drawings. Her devotion to this work, to the "wind-trail" of the "still, small voice within", became a model for mine, and I believe that of many other women and men I studied with. Could this trust be an intimation of Learning IV? What Jung called the "transcendent function", an ongoing acceptance of, and dialogue with, all images arising within experience, can finally lead to a form of simplicity and liveliness which Buddhists call "childlikeness". Here one lives creatively out of one's own astonishment with life, in an interactive community with others, without an overriding concern for convention or control. The performance of a healing reconciliation of self, other, and world are an ongoing, evolving effort counteracting a contrary process of splitting and dissociation. When done well, it may look effortless. Psychoanalyst Stuart Pizer imagines it this way:

> I picture the following metaphor for such a distributed self, in its dynamic straddling of multiplicity: a gymnast on a balance beam, apparently quite still, but maintaining the illusion of stillness through the constant negotiation of microadjustments among complex networks of muscle systems. (Pizer, 1996, p. 508)

Pizer suggests that a healthy sense of self balances and dialogues among "multiple islands of memory, affect, meaning, awareness, and intention," whereas a "damaged self" dissociates into "multiple subselves marooned on unbridgeable islands" (*ibid.*).

Susan Bach reaches back to the Cabbalah which tells a creation story in which vessels intended to hold God's light are not strong enough to contain it, scattering sparks of light throughout the world. In this myth, the work of human consciousness is to help gather the sparks, thereby participating in the construction of a healing divinity in everyday life. When we live far from such compassionate myth-making and self-reflection, we quench many sparks of light in ourselves and others. Then, our own personalities, as well as our hospitals and communities, lack healing ritual.

Bach wondered why it was that St. Francis of Assisi was such a powerful image for so many people, why he had such a hold on hearts and minds. Her answer could also apply to our admiration of Susan Bach:

> Is it his unselfishness, the freedom from the burden of worldly materialism, his devotion to the needy, his love for all living beings, tapping the neglected values of our own selves? Is he the complementary aspect to our own unlived life and deep longing? … What came to me at the end of my pondering was this: could it be that he heard God's voice and followed it, whereas we might hear it, but not follow it? (Bach, 1990, p. 93)

In raising such a possibility, Bach refers to what Jung has called the phenomenology of spirit. Jungian psychology, along with many non-Western healing systems, has recognized the possibility that there are unconscious self-organizing centres of symbolization and meaning creation within the psyche which are vastly superior to consciousness and outside its control. We connect with spirit when we are inspired by symbols, ideals, dreams, and feelings to move beyond old standpoints and see or act in new ways. One of the great joys of being a Jungian analyst is to witness the birth of such experiences in one's clients, as they are renewed by unexpected dream narratives or symbols which point to creative solutions for seemingly insoluble quandaries. In the realm of the spirit, we find oracles, prophecy, vision, and possession states. Jung believed that we need to remain in conscious dialogue with all such manifestations, leaving open the possibility of learning something new, while retaining critical judgement and a cautious analytical response. Spirit then yields a kind of knowable object that is almost the opposite of that of scientific method: not what is repeatable and independent of social context, but that which is unique, temporary, and local. From a point of view which sees psyche-soma-knowing-world as systemically connected, the numinous marginal can equally well be called unconscious, spirit, angel, or God. Learning IV, or the transcendent function, remains always balanced at the margin, open to synchronicity and new connections not previously noticed. The unconscious can then become a helper and develop in strength over time. Jung noticed this possibility:

Disalliance with the unconscious is synonymous with loss of instinct and rootlessness. If we can successfully develop that function which I have called transcendent, the disharmony ceases and we can then enjoy the favourable side of the unconscious. The unconscious then gives us all the encouragement and help that bountiful nature can shower upon man. It holds possibilities which are locked away from the conscious mind, for it has at its disposal all subliminal psychic contents, all those things which have been forgotten or overlooked, as well as the wisdom and experience of uncounted centuries which are laid down in its archetypal organs. The unconscious is continually active, combining its material in ways which serve the future. It produces, no less than the conscious mind, subliminal combinations that are prospective; only, they are markedly superior to the conscious combinations both in refinement and scope. For these reasons the unconscious could serve man as a unique guide, provided that he can resist the lure of being misguided. (Jung, 1953, p. 116)

It is important that we resist the impulse to project grandiose and inflated expectations of miracle cures toward our work with the unconscious. Jung is quite clear that spirit serves life, gives meaning to life, and finds its limit in life. Meaning and healing reinforce each other, but only up to a point. Living organisms also suffer, lose their way, and die. The important issue seems to be the attitude with which we make the journey. A pilgrimage, a voyage of discovery in a world where one can learn from and honour unknown sources, is perhaps a better metaphor for human explorers than an image of ghosts in machines.

Susan Bach's path has disappeared at our horizon, but she has left behind an important trail. Her work shows that expressive drawings can have a prospective function, as do other processes of living organisms. For those of us interested in the dynamic unconscious, she has opened a vast area of research in what will be, for many, unknown and unsuspected territories of meaning.

References

Bach, Susan (1990) *Life Paints Its Own Span*, Switzerland, Daimon 1990.

Bateson, G. (1972) *Steps Toward an Ecology of the Mind*, New York: Ballantine Books.

Gillett, E. (1998) Relativism and the Social Constructivist Paradigm, in *Philosophy, Psychiatry, and Psychology* **5**, 1.

Jung, C.G. (1953) / (1966) *Two Essays in Analytical Psychology* Collected Works 7, Princeton, NJ: Princeton University Press.

Jung, C.G. (1960) / (1969) *The Structure and Dynamics of the Psyche*, Collected Works 8, Princeton, NJ: Princeton University Press.

Machado, Antonio, From *Proverbs and Tiny Songs*, tr. Robert Bly in Bly, Robert, 1995 *The Soul is Here for It's Own Joy*, Hopewell, New Jersey: The Ecco Press. (p. 248)

Phillips, J. (1998) Commentary on Relativism and the Social Constructivist Paradigm, *Philosophy, Psychiatry, Psychology* **5**, 1.

Pizer, Stuart (1996) The Distributed Self, *Contemporary Psychoanalysis*, **32**, 4, p. 505.

4

Illness as Oracle: Psychosomatic Symptoms as Synchronistic Occurrences

by Kaspar Kiepenheuer

I dare to speak about something unspeakable. Much has been said and written[1] about the physical and spiritual background of psychosomatic manifestations, and yet the question whether they are synchronistic occurrences is unspeakable.

For some valuable suggestions that led me to my point of view I am indebted to Susan Bach (1990), Aniela Jaffé (1990), C. A. Meier (1986) and H. K. Fierz (1980). The most impressive insights, however, I received from my everyday teachers: the children and teenagers with whom I have worked, either as a doctor in the children's clinic, as a psychiatrist in the child-psychiatry clinic or today in my child- and teenage-psychiatry practice (where I also treat some adults).

Characteristics of Psychosomatic Illness

Psychosomatic sufferings are distress signals, expressing what cannot be expressed in any other way: hidden emotions breaking through. Rational measures of orthodox medicine are usually of little value in the treatment of psychosomatic suffering, at least for the total well-being of the ill person. Psychosomatic symptoms seem to be an intensification of a psychological energy to the point of physical manifestation. These illnesses can mean a bridge between body and soul, offering the affected person an approach to wholeness. Unfortunately, this bridge to a new orientation does not offer itself immediately and quickly. Rather, these physical messages are ambiguous, to be compared with answers of the *I Ching*.

---

[1] A version of this paper was first published in *Proceedings of the Twelfth International Congress for Analytical Psychology*, published by Daimon Verlag. Reprinted with permission.

The connections between body and psyche are not subject to a one-sided direction of cause and effect in which a specific emotional situation would call up a specific symptom. Rather we are faced with the typical question of "the chicken or the egg": psychophysical parallelism. When I see a child laughing I am not sure the laughter is because the child is cheerful, or if the laughter causes the child to be cheerful.

When a psychophysical symptom comes into existence a symbol is born. As a catalyst, the symbol can bring about a transformation in the spiritual as well as the physical area, if the meaning is understood. The literal understanding of symptom (from Greek) is "it falls together": coincidence, chance. If this falling together is connected with a symbol we have approached synchronicity.

Synchronicity

Synchronicity describes a subjectively significant coincidence, in time or space, of two or more separate occurrences or situations. Intellect may doubt a connection, but, on a feeling level, even the confirmed rationalist is strangely touched and may recognize that transcendent powers are involved. Such situations tend to happen during borderline experiences: illness, nearness of death, depression or other critical situations.

I do not wish to pursue the question whether these phenomena can be understood scientifically, except for the rather vague explanation that spiritual energies – emanating from a strong complex – become so intense that they influence the physical circumstances. Parapsychology has coined the term psychokinesis for comparable phenomena. Perhaps psychokinesis is very ordinary, although surprising. Immanuel Kant said: "That my willpower moves my arm is no more comprehensible to me than if someone were to say that the same would also be able to hold back the moon in its orbit." Is it outrageous to assume such long-distance effects? Those who believe in astrology recognize powers that are able to transcend vast spaces and times.

An example occurred for me during a study visit in London. While celebrating my birthday with a friend, an indescribable physical unrest grabbed me. I hurried back to my apartment where I received a telephone message that my father had died: a heart attack during a visit to a sun observatory high in the mountains of Mexico. He was a sun astronomer and had always talked of "his sun" with visible passion. Later, at home, I discovered next to his bed a 1947 booklet entitled *The Sun*, by Franz Masereel: it contained pictures of numerous wood engravings. One page was specially marked (Figure 4.1). The picture on it seemed to indicate my father's premonition of death. Only later did I learn about an old Mexican myth in which those dying are thought to unite with the sun. Apart from this collective aspect, I sensed my father's death as a personal message to me, since he "chose" my birthday as his "return home

Figure 4.1 Wood Engraving

to his sun". Thereafter we often met in dreams, where he developed a kind, fatherly tenderness toward me that had never existed during his lifetime.

From the estate of Aniela Jaffé a wonderful booklet from 1796 with the title *Ghost Appearances and Prophesies* came into my hands. I was astonished at the conjectures of the time: "If besides us there could not exist creatures that have such a subtle body that it could not be seen by our eyes in its natural form but that this merry body could be capable of giving itself more consistency from time to time, whereby it could be seen."

I think also about ghost stories, preferably English reports about ghostly apparitions. These ghosts seem to want to tell the living that they wander around unredeemed because something was not taken to a proper ending. For instance, there is the ghost that one could deliver by freeing the corpse from a wall. Thus, ghosts and related apparitions are to be perceived and taken seriously so that they can be freed from their boxed-in existence and buried properly, whether it be concretely or metaphorically.

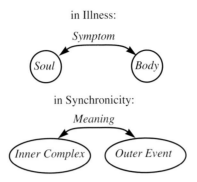

Figure 4.2 The Catalysing Function of a Symptom and of Meaning

What is the Common Factor?

The "subtle body" seems to approach a solution to the puzzle of psychosomatic and synchronistic events. In psychosomatic cases this subtle body corresponds to the symptom with its power of symbolism. The symptom represents a bridge between the unconscious and the ego through an unconscious content's choosing an expression that may become comprehensible to the ego. In synchronicity the meaning confronts us (see Figure 4.2). Here we experience a link, this time between the outer world and the inner. In both cases does this "subtle body" not approach that which Jung called the transcendent function?

A subtle medicine and psychology is needed to enable healing persons to make room for the transcendent function and to obtain a hearing for the "subtle body". All too often, this "subtle body" seems neglected in encounters with the ill, and there seems to be too little room for the work of the transcendent function. A free and yet protected place is needed for such qualities to constellate. I think of this place concretely in the therapeutic setting, but also in a transcendent sense, in that we cultivate a setting that leaves room for mysteries in the therapeutic process and the therapeutic relationship.

Charlotte

An experience with a girl's illness was valuable to me in becoming respectful toward the indescribable laws that I have tried to describe.

The girl's mother telephoned me. She was looking for help for her 12 year-old daughter, Charlotte, who was awkward, plump, lazy, an underachiever in school. Everything slid off her like raindrops off a taut umbrella. Among children she cut herself off in her own dreamworld. In school her sitting there "like a pudding" provoked the teacher. Already as an infant Charlotte was always hungry, while all others in the family – the parents and the three siblings – were slim, athletic and successful.

With me the slightly adipose girl seemed passive at first, but expectant. In the sandbox she stroked through the sand with her hands, mixed it, smoothed it and then cast a deep, questioning look at me. In the sand she created a peaceful scene with a farmyard, rural animals, a shepherd in the middle. "Like in paradise", she said. Then very suddenly, as if by magic, she held an enormous rubber monster over it: "With that it would not be so peaceful!" It was meant jokingly but we were both affected by this dark hint. At the parting after this first hour she pressed my hand for a long moment as if grateful.

Later she wrote a spontaneous composition that described her situation in a sympathetic way. Here is a shortened version:

The girl had been locked up with a mean woman for many years, because mother and father had died. She received bad food and all the mean woman did was scold the girl. The windows were barred. But one day the key was in the lock. With a smile on her face the girl quietly opened the door. The church clock struck and she knew she would soon be free. But she became very afraid of the cars outside because she did not know them. Briefly she thought: if only I had stayed inside the house! She lived on scraps. One day she met an artist who saw her pictures and invited her to live and paint with her. This is how she became a well-known painter. THE END!

At home, the sadder and quieter she became, the more the mother would scold her. She was imprisoned in a vicious circle. It was odd to learn that during pregnancy her mother had fungus poisoning and at the time of delivery had typhoid fever. Both left their marks on Charlotte s entrance into life. Did the prison stand for the connection with the "poisonous" mother in the physical as well as spiritual sense? I understood her cry for help for a place where a door opens, the church clock strikes and she can develop her true gifts. After her story it was understandable to me that the road to this goal was laborious. She said that it was so "terribly far" to my practice: in fact it was about 3 minutes.

In sessions with me, she was always "all there", involved and grateful for my being "there". In one sand-tray is a conical island (Figure 4.3); on top and in the middle is a man with a "loudspeaker" in his hand, "but it had no people" (that would listen): "maybe it was to lure the fish!" Behind him stands Tarzan with his hand raised (moral support?). Two waiters bring him something to drink, two women bring him something to eat. A policeman takes care of "the boats docking correctly".

Figure 4.3 Sandtray

Did Charlotte have to stuff herself because no one was really aware of her? Or the other way around: was she not more perceptible because she was shielding herself in this manner? It was as if ghostly apparitions were screaming for deliverance. The strengthening of this scream did not come from me as much as from her inner depth. Tarzan – expression of a primitive elemental force in her – supports the voice of the unheard singer. The first hint appears that she has found "her centre". At that time she had an angina accompanied by high fever. After that she seemed totally changed, as if she had incubated something in the warmth of the fever and the regression that was linked to it, and had blossomed out into an individual core of essence.

A tissue-paper collage (Figure 4.4) gives an impression of her outer as well as inner development of the time: a tender-fluffy flower with a dark sky and green ground. Just like the flower her face blossomed out. It was as if the mist in front of her eyes had lifted. In this way she could reach new horizons.

"Now we will make a holy landscape", she introduces her new sand-tray: the stable of Bethlehem. From there hay would be brought across two bridges to feed the sheep. The bell on the right would announce each time the arrival of the feed. This image gave me an insight into the true character of her hunger: a hunger for spiritual orientation.

In a later sand-tray (Figure 4.5), the strict separation of two contradictory worlds impressed me. On the left a tightly constructed town, on the right once again the stable of Bethlehem, this time with animals of different genera walking in a radiating formation, toward the Christ-

Figure 4.4 Flower

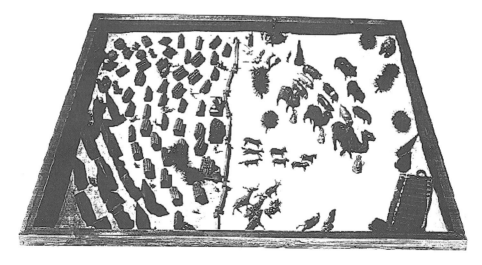

Figure 4.5 Stable

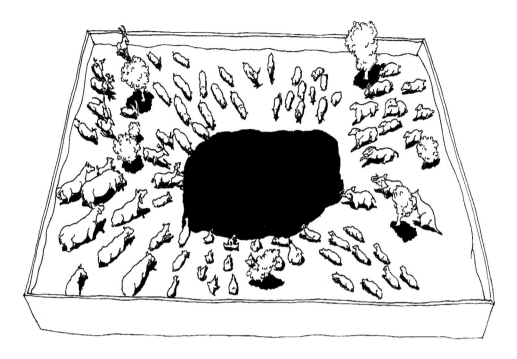

Figure 4.6 They are all thirsty

child. In between is a fence that "separates the two sides so that they will not disturb each other".

In school Charlotte had changed "like night and day", the teacher said. Her handwriting had improved in a striking way. The parents now took a totally different attitude toward the child; it remained unclear if it was the cause or result of Charlotte's changes. For all of us concerned, the connection remained as mysterious as the sound of the clock in Charlotte's story.

Our sessions became more comfortable. She chopped wood; I made a fire. She seemed to feel in good hands with me. She became more daring with the sand-trays; all of a sudden there is a monster "that surfaces there!", as if it belonged quite obviously in her life. I was glad to hear that she began a course in rock 'n roll and could make contacts spontaneously.

One last image in the sand (Figure 4.6) gave me a reassuring image of her soul. In the middle is a round lake, various animals come from all directions. "They are all thirsty" and drink from the lake. No animal seems disadvantaged; they are peaceful together. Contemplated as a whole, the image in the sand looks like a radiating sun – a convincing manifestation of the Self. And I felt a confirmation that therapy (after a year at this point) could now stop, as she urgently desired.

At a final conversation with the parents I wanted to share these impressive images. As if by a miracle, however, the slide projector "refused" several times. Synchronistically the projector gave me a sign: the secrets of the girl are to remain her own and she is to free herself from the influence of the parents. Simultaneously the parents were developing a respect, a stepping back from the Self of their daughter.

In a later composition Charlotte remembers the time of therapy: "I used to think that no one loved me ... that I was a dumb little girl .... Then I had to go to a psychiatrist .... During that time it was as if I was born a second time. It was as if the scales fell from my eyes."

These words summarise her history of suffering and healing. The recognition of her own values meant a new birth for her, comparable to a fish losing its scales, becoming a being of broad daylight.

To what degree did Charlotte's illness have synchronistic characteristics? Firstly, there was a physical and social illness on the outside and a suffering searching on the inside that pointed beyond the earthly "captivity" of the girl. Secondly, in the parents there was simultaneously a deviation of attitude that was associated (synchronistically?) with the illness of the child (Kiepenheuer, 1990). With the dissolution of the "ghostly apparitions" of the daughter the parents simultaneously gained a new attitude without my having to intervene – which would have created new feelings of guilt. Thirdly, a conventional attitude of cause and effect did not do justice to the girl in her situation. Rather a space had to be provided in which we could forget rational associations and let ourselves be surprised by entirely new dimensions. These at first seemed bizarre but later the transcendent, religious character emerged – in the holy birth and the sound of the church clock.

References

Bach, S.R. (1990). *Life Paints Its Own Span: Spontaneous Pictures of Severely Ill Children.* Einsiedeln, Switzerland: Daimon.
Fierz, H.K. (1980). *Jungian Psychiatry.* Einsiedeln, Switzerland: Daimon.
Jaffé, A. (1999). *Death Dreams and Ghosts.* Einsiedeln, Switzerland: Daimon.
Kiepenheuer, K. (1990). *Crossing the Bridge.* La Salle, IL: Open Court.
Meier, C.A. (1986). *Soul and Body.* Santa Monica, CA: Lapis.

5

Synchronistic Phenomena

by C. Toni Frey-Wehrlin

As Susan Bach was approaching the end of her life, she set up the Susan Bach Foundation and the Omega Foundation and entrusted both organisations with the task of furthering research into the "not-yet-known-but-knowable". My contribution to this tribute to Susan Bach pursues the same line of inquiry.

When Bach repeatedly referred to the fact, as borne out by her observations (Bach, 1990), that spontaneous drawings by seriously somatically ill children not only have diagnostic but often also prognostic significance, she found herself confronted with the problem of extrasensory perception (ESP). One aspect of ESP is precognition, and in the context of Jungian analytical psychology we refer to such phenomena as being *synchronistic*. The term synchronicity was first coined by Jung, who used the term to refer to a "principle of acausal connections" that encompassed all noncausal but meaningful coincidences, in particular phenomena such as clairvoyance, telepathy and precognition. Since Jung's first publications on the subject – in particular *On the Nature of the Psyche* (Jung, 1946) and *Synchronicity* (Jung, 1952) – a number of related publications have appeared, written principally, though not exclusively, by Jungian analysts. The contributions made by the physicist Wolfgang Pauli deserve particular mention. Pauli underwent Jungian analysis between 1931 and 1934, and remained in contact with Jung thereafter. Both researchers were interested in the relationship between their scientific fields, physics and psychology respectively. I refer the reader to their correspondence, which was published in 1992 (Meier, 1992).

These fields overlap especially clearly in the area of synchronistic phenomena. My overview, albeit very limited, leads me to presume that it is chiefly the leading exponents of the exact natural sciences who interest themselves in such phenomena and in the associated epistemological problems. (See for example: the correspondence between Pauli and Jung [Atmanspacher, *et al*, 1995]). It appears to be these same individuals who question – and seek to expand the limits of – the previously held principles of the sciences. Pauli's endeavours have been, and will continue to be, advanced on a broad front.

In contrast to this attitude, I am aware of the opinion of the large majority of the scientific middle-classes, among whom there appears to be some resistance to such an opening up. This resistance is given expression with the choice of adjectives such as "speculative", "dubious" and "unscientific".

I do not want to go into the possible reasons for this resistance here, but would like to express, however, the not-completely-unfounded suspicion that this resistance is, in turn, responsible for hindering the publication of observations into synchronistic phenomena. Thus we are faced with the paradoxical situation in which publication of scientific observations is obstructed due to "scientific" considerations. Some years ago a colleague of mine gave me a piece of friendly advice: delete any references to synchronistic events in your articles because "no one will believe you!"

Bearing this in mind I would, nevertheless, like to relate the following three experiences which have arisen during the course of my analytical practice (but not only there). It would seem that the time for a theory of synchronicity has not yet arrived, and is unlikely to do so before the necessary empirical work has been undertaken.

Case one

A twenty-five year-old musician sought analytical treatment in connection with a moderately bad depression, in addition to which he was suffering from somatic symptoms and a general life-crisis. After several months of analytical work there was an intensification of the patient's symptoms and a concurrent stagnation in the treatment. The situation became critical, with both patient and analyst experiencing a sense of hopelessness. The transference threatened to become negative and thus to jeopardise continuation of the therapy.

At this point the patient had the following dream:

A hero is climbing in a ravine, or shaft, searching for some treasure which he fails to find. The dreamer is with him. There appears to be no exit from the shaft. The dreamer climbs up some sort of chimney and finds a hatch at the top. This he does not open because although it would be big enough for him it would not be big enough for the hero. In addition to this he is aware that on the other side of the hatch there are bands of gangsters or police roaming about who would behave as belligerently towards the hero as towards himself. So both men remain in the hole.

The patient did not hesitate to interpret his dream as corresponding to his neurotic attitude. He could see how it related to the way things really were: there was evidently no way out of the hole he was sitting in. He fails to see that this "hero" is not a hero at all, but rather a "nobody" for whom he believes he must sacrifice himself. The patient's reasoning provides him with the big advantage that he can adopt the role of martyr starving in the underworld, not obliged to confront the big bad real world.

On a whim I asked him if he found it amusing to think of himself as Saint Sebastian, bound to a tree and shot with arrows. Completely astonished he then related a second dream:

> He is in the studio of an old sculptor. The man gives him a large cloth and asks him to use it to cover a statue of Sebastian which is standing in the corner.

It is quite common in analytical work that perfectly helpful, "positive" dreams crop up without yielding any beneficial development. On the contrary, when such dreams occur the patient tends to cling more tightly to his/her neurotic attitude. I think that in this case it was the synchronistic, "clairvoyant" idea, which came to me out of nothing so to speak, that shook the patient's resistance.

At any rate, both his depressive, disgruntled mood and his physical symptoms began rapidly to disappear, and various aspects of his life began to develop fruitfully. The patient suddenly found himself conscious of numerous, urgent problems. Problems he had to, and was now able to, confront. The spell had been broken and the ego had found its freedom once more.

Case two

This patient, in his mid-forties, was suffering from severe neurosis, and although this neurosis was characterised mainly by symptoms of depression, the presence of a bland psychotic process could not be entirely ruled out. The interesting association for us here arises from the patient's statement that he had always felt himself to have been "psychosexually raped" by his three year-elder sister. He realised, however, that this was merely his fantasy and that his sister had always treated him correctly.

Barely a year after he had started treatment, in November 1963, his sister paid me a visit – with the patient's consent – in order to inform herself of her brother's future prospects. On this occasion she also related a dream to me that she had had recently:

> At 3 o'clock in the morning my mother and brother break into our house with an almighty din .... They ask to be put up for the night. I find it very annoying but go about making up the beds anyway. My husband is standing sheepishly in the background.

I see this dream as being a counterpart to the brother's rape fantasy. In psychological terms one can talk of the brother and sister having a partial unconscious identity.

During the course of our conversation the woman described a second dream, which she had had eight years previously in 1955:

I am descending through a somewhat gloomy coniferous forest, down a wide, steep path towards the edge of the forest. There I see a large, cosy house bathed in golden light from the evening sun. Carved into the gable in large, clear characters is a date: *17 June, 1964.*

The dreamer felt this dream to be prophetic. As the date of the dream approached, she asked herself what she could expect.

Towards the middle of June 1964 she drove over the Julier Pass into the Engadine valley. She was thinking about the 17th, which was imminent, and it occurred to her that that day might be her last. The 17th fell during the holidays and nothing out of the ordinary occurred on that day. She had arranged to go hiking with a friend and the friend's husband. It was a hot day and early in the afternoon they were glad to be able to freshen themselves up in a cool mountain lake. They took it in turns to recite Goethe's "The Fisherman":

> The water murmured, the water rose,
> A fisherman sat on the side
> Silently watching his angling rod;
> And icy cold was his heart.
> And as he sat still and listened,
> The waters parted and rose;
> And out of the swirling waves appeared
> A water-nymph from below.
>
> "And why", she sang and she spoke to him,
> "Do you threaten my little ones so?
> If only you knew how happy it is
> For a fish to live in this river bed
> You would follow me down to live with us,
> Joyfully here below.
>
> Do not the sun, and also the moon,
> Reflect and draw strength from the sea?
> Do not their faces, in shimmering waves,
> Show beauty in higher degree?
> Are you not drawn by the lovely sky,
> Reflected in mystical blue?
> Does not your own face tempt you down
> Into th' eternal dew?"

The water flowed, and rose again,
And caressed his naked feet,
His heart overflowed with deep desire,
Such as when lovers meet.
She spoke again, and she sang to him
And his fate was sealed for ever:
Half pulled, half willing, he sank to the deep,
And seen again was he never.

Translated by Brigitte and Ronald Kay.

Back at her hotel the dreamer retired early and it was only the following day that she got the news that her brother had discharged himself from the clinic where he had been undergoing treatment for a physical illness. He had then gone to a lonely bank of a nearby lake and taken an overdose of sleeping tablets. He went into the water to die. The time of death was clearly ascertained as being between midday and three o'clock.

This case stands out in comparison to similar ones, firstly, because it was possible to transcribe the dream several months before the critical date; secondly, because a description of the events was given to me by an independent source (that is, by the friend who had accompanied the dreamer on the excursion).

Case three

This example is not drawn from analytical practice. The picture reproduced here (charcoal on paper, 80 cm x 58 cm) was drawn in 1972 by Beatrice Falk, who was 15 years old at the time. This picture is shown in Figure 5.1.

It depicts a slightly hilly landscape animated only by four pine trees, which are all more or less bereft of needles. In the foreground there is a large tree; its lower half is bare, while the upper part shows signs of growth. The remaining three trees are not only further away, but seem smaller – with the furthest appearing to be the smallest of the group.

The scene is lit from behind. The sun is directly behind the crown of the largest tree, surrounding it with a sort of halo. The sky is overcast, though one could imagine that it is brighter beyond the horizon.

Let me add a few dates from the life of the drawer subsequent to the execution of this drawing. In 1982 she found her long-term partner. They had three children, born in 1983, 1984 and 1989. Three months after the birth of the third child the father died unexpectedly due to complications following myocarditis. Initially the shock of his death had an almost paralysing effect on his partner, but after a year there was actually a surge of energy. The young woman, hitherto rather shy and reserved, discovered a totally new spirit of initiative and dynamism. She mobilised previously unused resources, acquired an unusually good flat, and, by putting her children in a day school, she was able to take a part-time job. In 1995 she stopped work and began a demanding long-term course of further education. The children have been in no way neglected as a result of these events however; on the contrary, their mother has striven for an intense and cohesive family life. Compared to her earlier – somewhat average – life, her life has now become exceptionally rich and fulfilling.

I would like to add a note to this third example. We are concerned here with paying tribute to Susan Bach, and I believe the case of Beatrice Falk to be "classic Bach": a spontaneous drawing, by a young person, that exhibits "forecasting signs" which cannot be overlooked.

Susan Bach was possessed not only of a creative mind, but also a critical one, and she was, if anything, more discriminating when appraising her own work than that of others. Although any impartial observer of our picture would doubtless find a connection between it and the subsequent fate of the drawer, we would do well to remain aware of the limited value of such prognostic evaluations if we are to avoid making unscrupulous prophecies.[1]

I see in the drawing a symbolic anticipation of the situation the drawer found herself in following the unexpected death of her partner. The half-bare trees standing in a completely empty and dismal landscape. The only "bright spot" – the halo formed at the top of the large tree by the half hidden sun – is, so to speak, from another world. It would be a misuse of the statement incorporated in the picture to claim that it enables one to foretell subsequent developments in the drawer's life. Unless one infers from the existence of a few remaining branches that there will be an abundance of new shoots in the future.

The same goes for many of the prognostic indications that Bach found in the pictures she published and upon which she commented. Thus she would, for example, always let it be decided first *ex eventu* whether three flowers signify three weeks or three months.

I have referred elsewhere and in depth to the fundamental differences between science and myth (Frey-Wehrlin, 1976). Science concerns itself with the *general, repeatable* (that is, by experimentation!) formulation of, and conformity to, natural laws. As Jung said to Bender: "Everything that can be repeated experimentally is necessarily causal" (Adler, 1873/1975, 6.3.1958). In contrast to which only myth can provide a true determination for *the individual.* Myth can supply an explanation for the same individual events that science would dismiss as coincidence. The millstone that strikes Mr. Korbes dead in Grimm's fairy tale represents both the punishment of God and the proof of Korbes' malice! According to Jungian typology one can also say that the instrument of science is thinking, and that of myth is feeling. Both belong to an integrated description of reality. As a rule one has to accept that these descriptions, or rather explanations, contradict one another. This is awkward, of course, and must be the reason for the aforementioned disquiet among many scientists. But as the physicist Hans Primas said:

---

[1] The same question is examined by Michael Edwards in chapter 11 [Editor].

70

Figure 5.1 Beatrice Falk's Picture

"A description is wrong the moment it is claimed to be the only correct one" (Atmanspacher, *et al*, 1995, p. 216).

Susan Bach was always wary of such arrogance and we would do well to follow her example by exercising the same caution.

Translation from the German by Bill Gilonis.

Note: Case one (Frey-Wehrlin, 1962) and Case two (Frey-Wehrlin, 1965) referred to above were originally published in another context and in a slightly different form.

References

Adler, G. (Ed.) (1973/1975), *C.G. Jung Letters*, Vol. 2, Princeton University Press.

Atmanspacher, H. Primas, H. Wertenschlag-Birkhäuser, E. (Eds.) (1995), *Der Pauli-Jung Dialog und seine Bedeutung für die moderne Wissenschaft*. Springer, Berlin Heidelberg, New York.

Bach, S.R. (1990), *Life Paints Its Own Span: On the significance of spontaneous paintings by severely ill children*. Daimon, Einsiedeln (Switzerland).

Frey-Wehrlin, C.T. (1962), Problems of Dream Interpretation, *Journal of Analytical Psychology*. 7, 132-140.

Frey-Wehrlin, C.T. (1965), *Ein prophetischer Traum*. In: Frey-Wehrlin, C.T. (Ed.), Spectrum Psychologiae. Rascher, Zürich, 249-251.

Frey-Wehrlin, C.T. (1976), Reflections on C.G. Jung's Concept of Synchronicity, *Journal of Analytical Psychology*, **21**, 37-49.

Jung, C.G. (1946) *On the Nature of the Psyche*. Collected Works, 1969, **8**.

Jung, C.G. (1952) *Synchronicity*. Collected Works, 1969, **8**.

Meier, C.A. (Ed.) (1992), *Wolfgang Pauli und C. G. Jung: Ein Briefwechsel*. Springer, Berlin. English: (Correspondence). To be published by Routledge and Princeton University Press.

6

Light out of Darkness; Towards a Personal Mythology

by Bill Burritt

On Mythology

It is interesting to note that, in looking for the derivation of the word, myth, the note in the dictionary says, "of obscure origin" (American Heritage Dictionary, 1969). That is most fitting, for immediately we are thrown into the unknown and the unclear, the area that I propose we explore. Of further interest is the fact that the definitions of myth reflect this obscurity. Here is a sampling of those definitions:

- One of the fictions or half-truths forming part of the ideology of a society.

- Any fictitious or imaginary story, explanation.

- A notion based more on tradition or convenience than on fact.

- In our considerations of myth, it is important that we keep in mind that myth, even in its derivation, has as a part of it the unknown, the vague, the obscure; it is important as well that we not project our ignorance onto the myth, that *it* is the incomplete entity, that *it* is not based on fact. What this definition points to is that it is based on fact that we do not understand. Other definitions seem to allow more of the uncertainty and the unclearness:

- A traditional story, originating in a preliterate society, dealing with supernatural beings, ancestors, or heroes that serve as primordial types in a primordial view of the world.

- Any real or fictional story, recurring theme, or character type that appeals to the consciousness of a people by embodying its cultural ideals or by giving expression to deep, commonly felt emotions.

In these definitions we note something that psychologically is closer to us; we know the experience of contents or expressions that mean something to us; we know the importance of certain kinds of celebration or ritual. We have a feeling for the observance of times of the year, times in life, places in history. Yet even these definitions seem to me to be inadequate: "in preliterate society" suggests that there is no current myth, and yet we would be hard-pressed not to find in the towers of commerce newly-formed expressions of meanings that once were carried by the spires of religious traditions, the pyramids of Egypt, the ziggurats of the Middle East and Mesopotamia. Similarly, in the array of movements which seek to express the nature of relationships, there are surely formulations of contemporary myth, the character of male and female, the various aspects of identity which are a part of us all. Where these definitions are on track is in the expression "commonly felt". Although there may be a mostly culturally-conceived reference here, I would suggest that, again from the psychological perspective, we have a statement that is tending toward the notion, not of a limited, unicultural orientation, but of the collective unconscious, of which the particular cultural experiences are expressions. This relationship between consciousness, its particular cultural expressions, and the collective unconscious is fundamental in analytical psychology, in the writing of C.G. Jung (1954a); it provides a significant theoretical foundation to what follows. With these preliminary considerations in mind, I would like to turn to some reflections on the collective face of mythology.

The Collective Face of Mythology

Before exploring this, I suggest that we have arrived at one of the premises of this paper, namely, that we begin as a part of something much bigger than ourselves, and that we begin without a sense of "we" or "I" at all. Who we are is wrapped up, contained, expressed in the anonymity of "non-I". Psychologically, we are referring to the unconscious, that we begin in a state of not-knowing; in Jung's writing, one of the expressions of this is *participation mystique*, the way in which, as part of the collective, part of the mass, there is nothing of the individual's voice or viewpoint. Developmentally, then, we can suggest that, in speaking of the ego function, it is a part of us that gradually differentiates from that mass and enables a growing sense of a separateness which allows the person to move along the path of autonomy (to use but one of the attempts to name the process of life).

As we have seen, there is a variety of definition of myth; what is now of greater significance is the function of myth. What purpose does it serve? What role does it play in the structure of the collective and individual psyche?

These questions lead us to a second premise. The function of myth is one of connecting us with the mystery of life in such a way that that mystery can be elucidated, and given shape and meaning. To the extent that this is so, myth as formed gives us indication of the ways in which our ancestors have striven to understand their experience of mystery. Myth as forming can enable us to give expression to our own experience of that mystery. In analytic thought, the myth is an expression or image of something that never can be known fully (this understanding is a very important aspect of the description of archetype); however, myth as both formed and as forming can be a vital resource in approaching and appropriating that "unknowable".

Let us return, then, to the collective face of mythology, for this is where we must begin, keeping in mind that we come into being as a part of the mass and the undifferentiated. Mythology is one of the voices which talks about this part of the mystery of our life. So it is that we read of the various accounts of the beginning of the world, of creation, of the various ways in which what we experience was introduced: in Greek myth, the way in which Prometheus challenged Zeus and brought fire to humankind; in native American myth, the way in which Diver brought up from under the water the bits of mud out of which was formed the land that we see. These accounts, at some point, for the people into whose culture they fell, had the kind of vitality that was sustaining and satisfying. That is to say, what we now call myth at one point carried the power of the religious expression which connected the people of that time to their roots in a way that was fitting for them. You will note here the connection I am positing between myth and the religious.

I feel it is important, even vital, to differentiate "the religious" from religion, for the latter is that which, at some time, expressed the felt vitality of the former. So it is that religion takes its multiplicity of form and expression; this diversity seems to indicate how important it is for religions to be related to the people and cultural setting in which they are found. I suggest that this growth and relatedness move, as with other psychic contents, from the unconscious to the conscious, that is, to the place where it finds the particular expression which meets the need of the individuals and groups concerned as they address the mystery of their lives.

Any religion may express the religious, or be only an empty shell from which the power, value, and meaning of the religious have fled. Perhaps myth can be considered in a similar light. That is to say, in its dynamic phase, the myth has this power of the religious in its ordering and reconnecting function, as it elucidates aspects of the mystery of life.

In light of this, it may be accurate to think of myth as "only a story" if, by that, we mean to convey that something of its dynamism has disappeared, that it does not carry the kind of power that the culture or group originally found to be so real and related. From another viewpoint, when myth is defined as "half-truth", it may be that the "half" that is missing is this very power to connect to the mystery of life; it has lost its connecting and relating function, and so become only story. "I don't believe in Santa Claus" is this kind of movement, and the adults around sometimes feel the loss of something which remains in the still potent, different perspective of the child.

It seems to me that myth needs to be understood from these two perspectives: one is the narrative aspect that enters into the oral and written tradition of a people or culture; the other is the dynamic aspect which speaks to and connects with the spirit and need of that same culture. This latter is the one which produces the art, the writing, the inspiration for life and movement. This is the creative energy which sometimes lies buried and inactive, but potentially dynamic, in the external forms and structures, institutions, and traditions of the culture.

This is the collective face of myth. Its locus is in the society, the country, the gathered tradition. And, when it is vibrant, it has the strength and force to express and carry the aspirations of those people. This is the meaning of "dynamic" as I am using it. The myth connects the people to the underlying sense of mystery and purpose which, I suggest, is at the heart and is the meaning of religious expression. It puts things in order, both those aspects of life that are clear, visible and comprehensible, and those that carry and express mystery, numinosity and wonder.

Paradoxically, the substance of myth is not created by that culture or those people. It is rather as if the collective unconscious erupts into the space and time which the culture occupies (Jung, 1958, p. 41[1]); it is then this content which is given form and shape in the subsequent works of that people. There is a correspondence, a relationship, between the unconscious stirrings, their eruption, and the ways in which the people, feeling that energy and its connectedness to something of themselves, give expression to it. We call these times eras or periods, characterizing them as Classical, Christian, Post-modern. In each of them there is a coming together of that part of the collective unconscious that is calling for attention, that in many ways forces its way into the conscious arena, and the capacity of the culture as a whole, or its accepted representatives, to express it and give it a shape in life.

An example: in this century there has been a tortuous winding movement in the sphere of relationship. From the perspective of analytical psychology, this has been thought of and formulated as the tension between the Masculine and the Feminine. I suggest that even the growth of the depth psychologies, with their emphasis on the exploration of the unconscious, was an expression of this tension, as Western culture had gone too far in the direction of rationalism, enlightenment, Masculine, Apollonian, thinking and behaviour. The collective unconscious was bound to erupt with an assertion of its place in the life of the collective psyche. The collective myth that was being lived out had to do with dominance and exclusive rightness of the rational, its capacity to solve everything and to achieve anything. This collective myth we continue to have to live with; it is not new. The instruction of Jahweh that man was to have dominion over nature is only one expression of its history and power. Into this overtly rational and Masculine field came a supreme expression of its very opposite, the unconscious, with its depth, its mystery, its terrifying images, and its own power. In this discovery there was unleashed the opposite of the collective, operational myth, the power of rationality and thought. There is no suggestion here of truth or untruth, validity or invalidity; rather, it is to recognize that this was the myth that drew and caught the allegiance and veneration of the

---

[1] Here Jung writes of "Metaphysical acts of cognition, that is to say, 'constellated' unconscious contents which are ready to erupt into consciousness."

collective; this was the object of worship. During this century we can see the way in which this myth formed such a powerful focal point on the one hand, and the way in which the unconscious also provided something that was to redress the imbalance. We have called it by a thousand names, but the focus of them all has been, and is, to bring into the conscious sphere the Feminine as an equally important aspect of the life we live. It is painfully clear that we have a long way to go.

Mythology and its Relationship to the Religious

When I use the words religious or spiritual, it is important to understand that I am meaning something quite different from what might be conveyed if we were to talk about religion. For the religious or spiritual has to do with the impressions, senses, and perceptions of the nature of life in its diversity, mystery, and wonder. Religion, I suggest, is the attempt to order that experience, to put into common language that which in fact begins in an unknown place and comes to us uninvited. I an convinced that the religious is a natural expression, a facet of who we are as human beings. This, for me, is very much related to Jung's articulation of the religious instinct (1954b, p. 83). Arising from that fact, we have the multitude of expressions which are attempts to give voice, form, and substance to what is essentially mystery. Some of these expressions we call religion. We might say, then, that religion is the presented face of the mystery, the face that has the affirmation of conscious, collective opinion. And for a very good reason: the affirmation is there because the religion still expresses the religious content which has emerged into that time and space. The wintry, dark time of year is a prime example as we look at the various religions which find in that season a phenomenon which speaks to the tension between darkness and light, polarities which can be understood in so many ways. Christianity, to cite but one of those, is at least an expression of the emergence of that kind of spirit, in the person of Jesus, which was born, lived and taught. The time was "right" to such an extent that its spirit has maintained its vitality over generations and centuries. For some, that spirit lives on; for others (and this has always been the case in the Christian era and, I suggest, in any era or place where there has been a dominant expression of the religious), the vitality was never there, or the vitality has gone out of that particular expression. This need not be a surprise to us, nor need it create any great distress, for what we observe in the interplay between the religious, and the religions which express it, is archetypal in nature. We can, with Jung, differentiate here the archetype, the form which is in itself unknowable, and the archetypal image, the content, which gives some glimpse of the archetype in its partial presentation of the whole. No "religion" will ever, or can ever, express the fullness of the religious in life. Each one, with its adherents, through its particular content, ritual, and dogma, can express something of great importance, and, as such, needs to be highly valued for the wealth it can bring into life. Not any of them needs to be elevated to the position of the supreme and only expression capable of capturing what is experienced as religious. In the history of religion we can see clearly the ways in which, as with empires, there is rise and fall, even as with respiration there is inspiration and expiration, expressions of life and death. As we welcome the death of an autumn and winter in the hope of a spring and summer, so we might welcome the demise of the forms of religion which need to die so that a successor might express in a more satisfying manner and form the aspirations, experiences, values, and insights of the individual and the group.

Mythology shares much with this way of grappling with the relationship between the religious and religion, for it too has had its dynamic, contributing phase, along with the time when, as a dynamic force, it has died. The classical stories of Mediterranean cultures were not, for their adherents, stories alone, any more than for a committed Christian is the story of the Cross a story alone. In both instances there is present a power which spoke to and convinced the spirit of the adherent, a value which was so because the images which were conveyed to the adherent and the group ordered and connected their experience to the numinous and the unknown, It is for this reason that we speak of mythology as "just a story" at our peril, for we may be losing a form and expression that best conveys the mystery of life, and perhaps even some of its resolution.

The Collective / Individual Tension

I have been referring to mythology, to the greater extent, from the perspective of the collective. And it is understandable for that to be the starting point, for it is in the collective that we begin, and particularly, it is in the collective conscious orientation that our early values and sense of identity are shaped. This same orientation exerts the kind of power which compels us to be like the groups in which we find ourselves. It is important to affirm the value of these beginnings; however, equally important is to pay due regard to the multi-valency of those beginnings. We come into life with no conscious sense of who we are; the societal and familial structures and relationships, our experience of nature, our exposure to a wider culture, all of these potentially extend to us the external holding contexts in relationship to which our latent and nascent essential personality can find expression.

The significance of these contexts cannot be overstated, regardless of their quality. And inevitably, there will be different quality: the kinds of parenting which are characterized by absence, presence, holding, suffocating, abuse, caring, encouragement (giving heart) or fear; social groups which may be open, exclusive, dogmatic, inviting, thoughtful, repressive, dynamic, or stifling. Into this variety of conflicting stances we all come with the potentiality to become who we are, including who we are in relationship to that history and setting which we enter. So it is that we begin to shape our personal mythology, and simultaneously to have it shaped by the collective settings of which we are a part.

It is the collision of these personal and collective directions which contributes so significantly to the fulfilment of an individual life. Such can be the strength of the collective, operational, dominants, the myth of the collective, that the inevitable collision wipes out the personal; the individual may then never come to her/his own life. Such a collision calls for the greatest resources of the one concerned to withstand and come to terms with that collective dominant power, not necessarily to overcome or defeat it, but certainly to assign it to its proper place in the psychic economy. It may continue to live in the house, but it must not take over all the rooms.

This kind of collision may be repeated, even as the labours of Herakles are twelve in number. This repetition points both to the power that is being encountered and to the necessity of keeping one's personal, and personally understood, myth alive; it is the stuff of an individual life.

It seems that the early years hold the embryo of this individual myth; it is the time of greatest vulnerability, the time when the developing young one is most reliant on the groups and settings that form the encircling society. It is this encircling which provides the possibility of creative holding, a holding which expands and stretches as the developing one grows. Yet the encircling has within it another potentiality, that of confining and retarding any development, often because of the fear that the young one may be bringing some new and unsettling qualities or perspectives. Separation is what is being encountered here. For the established one, there is the potential separation from the known, the understood, with all the security which these hold, in addition to the values which they convey. As well, there is the separation of the neophyte, the act of leaving the group and social identities, with all the attendant risks in finding out what it is like to be "alone".

Both of these perspectives are included in the movement toward, and the formation of, this personal myth. It seems to me that one way of reflecting on psychic health is to consider it in relation to the extent of the individual's having been able, through personal resource and collective encouragement, to appropriate that personal myth. Psychic unhealth may be described as the loss of that mythology.

In analytical psychology, there is the understanding that where a particular psychic influence becomes too one-sided, the psyche takes some action to redress the over-emphasis. When one side of any question is being addressed, it means that there is a shadow side, that something else is not being paid the kind of attention it deserves or is calling for.

Mythology, by its very nature, seems to be a wide and collective expression of the mysteries. Stories of creation, the various ways in which life has evolved into what we know, having left behind the broken utopias in which only gods, or gods and unadulterated humans, lived in harmony, these are accounts which talk of the human condition; these are accounts which express the archetypal base of life which, through their multiplicity and uniqueness, shed different rays of light from different angles, so that varied faces of life are illuminated. Those myths, and others which sketch the broad details of life, are marvellous, as they express the mystery and the themes of the unknown, the processes through which humankind has come to be alive and to shape that living.

This aspect of mythology carries a very high value, serving a great purpose, for it unites us with history, not only in regard to time, but also in regard to being human. It unifies us, as it offers the link to the experientially-based wisdom of the ancestors. It can be seen in the wonder of curiosity in regard to creation, cosmos, the regions beyond, the regions under. These curiosities become disciplines or hobbies or vocations; they all carry something of the accumulated wisdom and push for fresh understandings.

This understanding must move from its collective beginnings if it is to be plumbed for the fullness of the riches it can offer. And it probably does this in the voice, writing, craft, or teaching of those who are struck by, and respond to, its power. So the Apostle could write:

> Something which has existed since the beginning,
> that we have heard,
> and we have seen with our own eyes;
> that we have watched
> and touched with our own hands:
> the Word, who is life –
> this is our subject.

> (I John 1:1, The Jerusalem Bible)

Throughout history we can see and hear the persons and voices who articulated the newest expression in myth; who, in turning the diamond body, revealed an additional aspect which sparked into life. These are the moments when the boundaries are pushed back or stepped over, when humankind has, perhaps through the agency of one person, the opportunity to be more than it is and has been. We call it art, bravery, courage, creativity, insight.

If life is anything, it is tension. It is a pulling in the other direction even as we value the qualities just mentioned. Life wants stability and unchange – a stasis which asks no questions, which rests unchallenged. So it is that, when one dares to ask, a significant power in the collective often says "No", sometimes by fighting the new, sometimes by wrapping the new up so tightly in the earlier collective values that it cannot breathe. A myth says it in this way:

> Cronus married his sister Rhea, to whom the oak is sacred, But it was prophesied by Mother Earth, and by his dying father, Uranus, that one of his own sons would dethrone him. Every year, therefore, he swallowed the children whom Rhea bore him: first Hestia, then Demeter and Hera, then Hades, then Poseidon.
> Rhea was enraged. She bore Zeus, her third son, in the dead of night ....

> (Graves, 1955, p. 39.)

Even as there is here the expression of "no-saying" to life, so there is the activation of the opposite pole, the one which, energized and dynamic – "Rhea was enraged" – brings something new to life, born in the place where we do not see or know of its presence. So it is in the workings of the unconscious as seen in analytic work. "A child is born," says a dream, and it can often be seen and experienced how the analysand has been unknowingly pregnant with this possibility, conceived months before.

Quite frequently, this "no-saying" may be characterized as the conserving and conservative pull of collective orientation; this is often the face it presents. I think that it may be more advisable to describe it as the conservative aspect of the unconscious itself, of which the collective orientation is the presenting medium.

Towards a Personal Mythology

The collective mythology is what we know best and most easily. From whatever direction we approach, the collective is present and strong; its strength lies in its capacity and nature to overcome the particular and the unique. This strength can be seen in any place, situation, institution, gathering, where there is an implicit or explicit value attached to the individual's being primarily "a part of" the mass, part of the group. It can be seen where there is unquestioned support for the cause, the structure, for "the way things have always been". The power of this is seen in the Greek myth of the father gods who, in various ways, conceived their children, only subsequently to go about the task of making sure that they were not allowed to grow to maturity.

It is in contrast to this, and developed from it, that I suggest the immense importance and value of the personal myth, the articulation of a personal mythology, for it is in this that the potential uniqueness and particularity of the person can be affirmed, nurtured, and seen. And what does a personal mythology look like? Here are some ways of describing it so that, if it is met, we might have a chance of recognizing it.

A personal myth is not automatic, assumed, or inherited. The nature of one's own myth is not received, formed and shaped, from those who have gone before, regardless of the gifts and resources those others may have had, and even made available. It cannot be put on like a new outfit or costume, for I suggest its place of origin must be from within, even when the various inklings about it may be, and often are, seen in outer life. It involves not simply a receiving of the gifts and accidents of one's history, but a grappling with those so that they may be located fittingly in the life of the individual. This will involve some rejection, some acceptance, of overvalued and undervalued aspects of life and experience.

We can recognize the presence of a personal myth in the experience of uncertainty and ferment, because a developing personal myth constrains the participant to work, often to agonize; the words passion and patience share the same root word which means to suffer. These two are necessary qualities – the willingness to be passionate, affectively involved, and patient, enduring the times of silence, waiting, and stillness – in the refining (I originally wrote "refinding") process of one's life and direction – one's myth. Personal myth compels us to ask the questions which may never have been asked, or, if posed, have been answered all too easily by collective opinion, value, and orientation. Very rarely, it seems to me, is a personal myth to be found in the standpoints of collective consciousness. It may be recognized in the presence of more suffering, for often what is held to be the most sacred and revered has its primacy of value questioned and, at times, rejected, in the on-going process.

It always has to do with something lost. In becoming who we are, the collectivities of life form a tremendous foundation; personal myth calls these foundational formations into question; personal myth calls the individual to a knowledge of where s/he wants to stand and, at times, not wanting to, but having to. Again and again the individual is, like Odysseus, pushed out into the "wine-dark sea", an image which speaks to me of a refining process, as the wind and waves of inner and outer life shape the person's very being, not simply in terms of the externals, but of the psyche itself. The issue that in one moment seems to have been resolved suddenly changes its face slightly and confronts the traveller again, subtly yet powerfully differently.

It is impossible to describe it fully; there are countless ways in which we might have a sense of the personal myth forming and taking shape: the intuitive impression, the chance encounter, the synchronistic events, the retrospective thoughts in which valuable links and meanings are seen and felt in new and dynamic ways, even when there may have been the sense of having been over this territory before. It may be found in the idea that will not allow any resting, the book that has to be read.

In the paying attention, in the respect for the experience of life that ordinarily might be rejected, in these the personal myth makes itself visible and asks to be shaped.

References

The American Heritage Dictionary of the English Language (1969). American Heritage Publishing Company Incorporated and Houghton Mifflin Company, Boston.

Graves, Robert (1955). *The Greek Myths*. Penguin Books, London.

The Jerusalem Bible (1966). Doubleday: New York.

Jung, C.G. (1954a). *Two Essays an Analytical Psychology*. Vol. VII of the *Collected Works of C.G. Jung*. Bollingen Foundation, Princeton University Press: New York.

Jung, C. G. (1954b). *The Development of Personality*. Volume XVII of the *Collected Works of C.G. Jung*. Bollingen Foundation, Princeton University Press: New York.

Jung, C.G. (1958). *Answer to Job*. Bollingen Foundation, Princeton University Press. New York.

Picasso's Minotaur Series Reconsidered in the Light of Animus and Anima

by Ralph Goldstein and Barbara Harborne

Introduction

When Susan Bach was completing the English version of *Life Paints Its Own Span* (Bach, 1990), she was surprised by how many of the essentials of "Inner Knowingness" were foreshadowed in the Ciba Geigy Monograph of 1966/69 (Bach, 1969). But among the new ideas worked out in *Life Paints its Own Span* was the application of her method of observation – the Zürich method, as it could perhaps be called[1] – to works of art. Specifically, she successfully addressed the vexed question of the ordering of the series of tapestries in the Musée Cluny, known as *La Dame à la Licorne; the Lady and the Unicorn* (see chapter 16).

What we intend to do here is to use the essentials of this method to show how Picasso's series of engravings on the theme of the Minotaur can shed light on the anima-animus syzygy and in turn how these archetypal symbols shed light on this puzzling series. In one of those coincidences, in which Jungians (certainly Susan) have learned to delight, Hans Bach, Susan Bach's husband, wrote a neglected, but scholarly and enlightening paper, called *On the Archetypal Complex: His Father's Son* (Bach, 1973). We have relied heavily on this paper for research on Dionysos, bulls and the Cretan Minotaur.

There is another reason for writing about Picasso, which seems highly appropriate in a volume dedicated to the memory of Susan Bach. She hoped that her book might testify to the light C.G. Jung threw on her own life's path (Bach, 1990, p. 97). We will attempt to amplify Jung's review of a Picasso retrospective show in Zürich in 1932 (Jung, 1984). Here Jung wrote about the light and the dark anima as symbols in Picasso's works and the process of splitting

---

[1] We are thinking of the role of co-workers, such as Hans-Peter Weber; see chapter 2 in *Life Paints Its Own Span*.

("schizoid") involved in wrestling with such conflicts, as depicted in Picasso's work, even before the Minotaur series. In paragraph 108, he wrote of his clinical observations:

> Among patients, two groups may be distinguished: the *neurotics* and the *schizophrenics*. The first group produces pictures of a synthetic character, with a pervasive and unified feeling-tone. ... The second group ... produces pictures which immediately reveal their alienation from feeling. At any rate they communicate no unified, harmonious feeling-tone, but, rather, contradictory feelings or even a complete lack of feeling. ... The picture leaves one cold or disturbs one by its paradoxical, unfeeling and grotesque unconcern for the beholder. This is the group to which Picasso belongs.

(N.B. The italics are in the original. A footnote was added to make clear that Jung was not diagnosing Picasso as a schizophrenic. Also we should probably understand this term to mean a psychotic process.)

This has been much misquoted; see for example, Gedo (1980), who mistakenly takes Jung to be diagnosing Picasso as psychotic.

Picasso has reached the status of one of the greatest painters of this century in large part because of the pioneering artistic movements which he led. But, as Chipp (Chipp, 1988) has pointed out, when artists portray eternal problems of living they tend to speak to us all. Neumann has gone further and made the case for art being part of the transcendent function, effective in all of us, with great force:

> The need of his times works inside the artist without his wanting it, seeing it, or understanding its true significance. In this sense he is close to the seer, the prophet, the mystic. And it is precisely when he does not represent the existing canon, but transforms and overturns it that his function rises to the level of the sacral, for he then gives utterance to the authentic and direct revelation of the numinosum.

> (Neumann, 1959, p. 97; see also pp. 93-94)

It then becomes a question, not of analysing the artist's life or psychology, but of analysing the work taking into account important biographical information and relating the work to wider symbols and contexts, such as aspects of the archetypal. This is a rather different undertaking to the work of Gedo (1980), who tried to use the work as biography, to make hypotheses about Picasso's state of mind. In short, the difference we are emphasising is that between amplification and association in the analysis of dreams.

Interestingly, towards the end of writing this paper, we have found two papers in German by an analytical psychologist on Picasso's *Minotauromachie* (Seckel, 1959, 1973). These early papers made reference to some of Jung's writings, but not to the paper on Picasso. Nevertheless, Seckel has concentrated on the notions of archetype, shadow and animus-anima. In the earlier paper, Seckel suggested that the figures which are represented in particular in the *Minotauromachie*, which will be discussed below,

> … are archetypes of the human soul. They present us with a key to the forces which most strongly held him in thrall. Viewed through the biography of the artist, they point to definitive persons. (Translated by Brigitte Kay.)

There is an increasingly rich literature on the archetypal concepts of animus, anima and shadow; e.g. Hillman (1985) and Ulanov and Ulanov (1994). The Ulanovs make many references to theological and literary sources, but very few to visual ones. Hillman's rich and scholarly work on *Anima* was designed to provide grounding for the vision of soul in psychology (see Preface, x). Works of art can contribute to our understanding of Hillman's sub-title, *An Anatomy of a Personified Notion*, by providing images and instances of such personifications, as we will try to show.

The Minotaur Series of Engravings

Picasso is especially interesting, because he combines the creative, inspirational, muse-like characteristics of anima with the obviously erotic and more narrowly sexual aspects, in a wealth of pictorial imagery and movement. We also have available a great deal of biographical and critical material. Picasso's first use of the figure of the minotaur was for the Surrealists' magazine *Minotaure 1* in 1933 (See Penrose, 1991, p. 16). As Baer so clearly put it (Baer, 1997, p. 14), the minotaur was "a 'found object' which allowed him to speak of all the contradictions in human behaviour: body / soul, devil / angel, human / animal". But the image obviously worked in him for he took it over and transformed it in many ways; psychologically, the image of the minotaur constellated archetypal aspects of one or more complexes in Picasso that are relevant to us all.

Picasso's lifelong friend, Sabartés, suggested that if we could only reconstruct his itinerary step by step, "we would discover in his works his spiritual vicissitudes, the blows of fate, the satisfactions and annoyances, his joys and delights, the pain suffered on a certain day or at a certain time of a given year" (Gedo, p. 253).

In a cycle of exactly two years, between the dates 17th May 1933 and 3rd May 1935, Picasso produced at least 22 etchings with the figure of a Minotaur, varying from outline drawings to the very large and heavily worked *Minotauromachie* (1935), probably his most famous etching. The *Minotauromachie* is usually considered as a major precursor to *Guernica* in terms of iconography (e.g. Chipp, 1988, Blunt, 1969). We will show that there is another engraving, of the same size as, and similar complexity to *Minotauromachie*, which both illuminates this better-known work and also prefigures *Guernica*. This work is known as *The Great Corrida with Female Matador* (1934) and is reprinted here as Figure 7.1 (p. 91).

Picasso produced large numbers of works concerning bulls, horses and matadors, motifs taken from the *Corrida*. The Minotaur transcends that environment as we shall see. But why work with animal forms? Chipp (1988, p. 52) put it very succinctly:

> In view of Picasso's propensity for endowing his favourite animals, the bull and the horse, with human emotions and even human resemblances, it should come as no surprise to find the frequent merging of animal and human characteristics. Indeed, in a true surrealist spirit, transformations between humans and animals could take place from either side or could exist in constant metamorphosis.

In working with dreams and other material, analytical psychologists make use of the idea that animals carry projections of the instinctual, emotional sides of ourselves – anthropomorphism. Clearly it is possible to reverse the direction of this projection and then to introject actual or imagined animal qualities into humans – theriomorphism. Here the image of the minotaur (and the horse and bull) will be particularly instructive. The relationships between human and animal, soul and instinct, male and female, sex and love are eternal questions.

A further important aspect of these dilemmas is their two-sidedness; it is not as if one can always maintain *a priori* which is "good" and which is "bad"; which is light and which is dark. Thus, as Jung pointed out in his review of 1932, we see reflections of the light *and* dark anima in Picasso's work. Symbols always seem to have this dynamic capacity for two-sidedness.

Some Biographical Background

The relevant biographical details are Picasso's age, his relationships with his then wife and mistress and their children and / or pregnancies. Picasso was born on 25th October 1881 and died 8th April 1973. He married the Russian ballerina, Olga Koklova, in 1918. She bore their son, Paulo, in 1921. By approximately 1927, Picasso was involved with Marie-Thérèse Walter, a much younger girl, born about 1910 (Gedo, 1980)[1]. During this relationship he produced some beautiful, erotic pictures with clear references to Marie-Thérèse as model. An example is *The Dream (Woman asleep in an Armchair)* of 1932. Penrose (1991) refers to the ideas of Jung with a parallel to this picture, called *Girl before a Mirror*, 1932, in which a female figure, modelled on Marie-Thérèse, is gazing into a mirror; a mirror of this type is called a *psyché*, so she gazes into her unconscious. It seems likely that in the artist's fascination with this subject, he is also wrestling with reflections of his creative muse as she works on *his* unconscious.[2] Marie-Thérèse bore a daughter, known as Maya, on 5th September 1935. She was named

[1] Chipp (*op. cit.* p. 59) gives the date of the meeting as 8th January 1927.
[2] This might be one way of understanding the "Artist and his Model" series of Etchings; see Baer (1997) and Picasso's Vollard Suite (1956).

Maria Concepcíon, which were the names of his two sisters and close to Marie of Marie-Thérèse. His relationship with Marie-Thérèse was deteriorating when he met Dora Maar in the middle of 1936.

It is well established (e.g. Gedo, 1980 and O'Brian, 1976) that Picasso's relationship with Olga had been very difficult for some time and they separated on 12th July 1935, their wedding anniversary. A very important issue was whether or not, under French law, Olga was entitled to half of his paintings. It has also been much commented upon that this period was relatively lacking in creativity by Picasso's standards, especially in painting (Gedo, 1980 and Chipp, 1988). Thus scholars appear to have suggested that this was a fallow period, at least in terms of numbers of works produced, but we intend to show that the etchings we are discussing here are exceptionally rich in imagery significant to the artist. It is important to note that by the date of Picasso's separation from Olga, Marie-Thérèse was approximately seven months pregnant and that the relationship had lasted as much as eight years. An impending illegitimate birth would have been all the more unwelcome, given the Catholic background in Spain and France and the fact that Picasso was still legally married. Olga's experience of her pregnancy with Paulo (see Gedo, 1980) meant that Picasso had particular reason to fear the possibly extreme emotional effect of pregnancy on the mother-to-be.

Jaffé (1988) refers to this period as a time when Picasso developed a "wholly personal mythology" (p. 104), albeit acknowledging that he had been working with many classical myths in illustrating Ovid's *Metamorphoses* and Aristophanes' *Lysistrata*. We will show that this mythology / iconography transcends the personal. However, in relation to light and dark and the mood of the times, Jaffé draws our attention to a painting of 1934, entitled *Bullfight* (opposite p. 104) [Oil on canvas, 38" x 51"]. The bull is dark and the horse is light and as usual the horse is succumbing to the charge of the fighting bull. The background lightly sketches the sense of watching faces in the stands and is strongly related to some of the backgrounds in the etchings, possibly including the profile of Marie-Thérèse as Picasso represented it. However, there are no matadors or picadors.

There is a smaller painting, which predates the *Bullfight*, called *Death of the Female Torero in the Corrida*, dated 6 September 1933 [oil and crayon on wood], which is lighter in mood and much less abstract in style. A less fearsome bull has nevertheless tossed and gored a white horse over its back. The horse, which unusually is male, carries the virtually naked, lilac coloured, torera prone across its back, arms towards the horns. This composition appears to be the basis of the etchings discussed below, especially the relationship of horse and female matador.

Mythology of the Minotaur

The basic story of the myth of the minotaur (e.g. Larousse Encyclopedia of Mythology, 1959) is well-known. In the time of the mother goddess, the male element was known to be sacrificed in underground ceremonies, such as the slaying of a bull in Crete, whose blood flowing into the ground was held to promote and renew the fertility of the earth.

Dionysos, son of Zeus (from his thigh), married Ariadne (a Mother Goddess representation), who was left on Naxos by Theseus, who had slain the Minotaur with the help of Ariadne. She provided him with a sword and a skein of red thread to find the way back from the labyrinth. Dionysos also has a bull form.

Dionysos is the god of the phallus and may be evoked as a bull. But he is unique among all the gods of the Greek pantheon, in that the symbols associated with him seem to conceal rather than reveal a consistent figure. He is not simply a chthonic fertility demon. Hans Bach wrote on p. 13:

> Dionysos is indeed the god of the phallus, but he is not worshipped as the source of human procreation, not mentioned in relation to marriage or the organisation of the family or tribe, of communal life or law. Wheat is sacred to him, but he has no link with agriculture.

Dionysos was also the god of prophecy and prophetic dreams, but in his theriomorphic form as a bull, Dionysos is still below the human level, yet also in a sense above, because animals are carriers of divine qualities (and of the sun). The bull (and goat) are symbols of creative power on an earthbound level, still undifferentiated, of "the animal within" and "the instinctual forces". Such a form presents something of an opposite to the notion of animus with its reference to logos, the conscious word.

Picasso is clearly working with chthonic images which emerge from the Shadow, or underworld. Viewers have continued to be moved by these etchings, but is there something universal in the way that their emotions are engaged?

Examination of the Works

There is a series often referred to as the "blind minotaur series" of four etchings and another series of more bacchanalian etchings. The *Minotauromachie* can be seen as the linchpin of both, since it incorporates aspects of both series. We will examine the most complex and carefully worked etchings, but we do not want to diminish the relevance of those etchings which we have omitted. The minotaur metamorphosed through many forms in Picasso's work; sometimes he was playful and loving, sometimes rapacious and sometimes pathetic. These changes through polar opposite moods parallel the general observation that symbols are always two-sided (Jung *et al*, 1964).

Generation and Death

We can begin with a very large etching, which does not in fact contain a minotaur, but does portray the themes of the *Corrida* and the *femme torero* image. This etching is the same large size as *Minotauromachie* and very detailed; it clearly commanded Picasso's attention and energy. The title[1] is *The Great Corrida with Female Matador* presented in Figure 7.1. Baer (1997) refers to this as one of Picasso's finest prints, but it does not receive comment elsewhere, as far as we are aware. In the centre is a raging bull, drawn with exceptional attention to its furious face. The lines of the horns are neatly echoed in the bull's penis and one horn looks as though it is deliberately drawn to thrust between the legs of the woman. All the other protagonists are female, except perhaps for the amorphous figures in the background. (See Fierz-David, 1988, for a discussion of such figures as souls.) The horse is almost always female in Picasso's iconography (Chipp, 1988). There is a large-breasted female matador across the back of the bull, with her neck and head arched high as she exhales; perhaps her soul leaves with her dying breath (see chapter 14, On the Relationships between Psyche and Soma, in Bach, 1990, especially pp. 124-5 and figure 126, *The Death of Prokris*).

And yet she may be painfully alive and she is perhaps pregnant, if one looks carefully at the line of her belly. Close by the navel is a hook-like shape, which could be a (reversed) 'P' for Picasso. We might be tempted to speculate that (more ambiguously) an abstracted tortured head nestles under her bosom, even Picasso himself, and furthermore, that this is Marie-Thérèse across the bull. We know there was indeed a raging battle between Picasso and Olga during these times, which has been well-documented (O'Brian, 1976), so that we could speculate instead that the female matador is Olga. The range of possibilities for what is represented in this etching are still a matter of conjecture, but the furious, crazed mood is unmistakable.

Across half the picture is an enormous lance carried in a relatively feeble arm by a rider who is hidden behind his protected horse, most unusually shown wearing the padded covering known as the *peto*. The horse's head is a direct precursor of the horse's head in *Guernica* and may be compared with plate 9 in Chipp's book (*op. cit.*). This horse has staring eyes, wide-open mouth and its mane stands on end; it is a picture of terror. This lance continues to the middle of the forehead of the female figure with Marie-Thérèse's silhouette. In this position, it is reminiscent of the *uraneus* – the serpent on the head-dress of the pharaohs. Of course, Marie-Thérèse was "the other woman", the betrayer, but also the creative muse / anima-figure.

It is important to note that the lance, albeit extended from the calm-faced Marie-Thérèse, does not penetrate the matador, but rather the bull behind the horns and between the shoulders. This is the place of the killing thrust made by the matador. In front of the horse's

---

[1] It was rare for Picasso himself to name his pictures, so we should not read much into titles. However, it is likely that viewers have been misled in their looking as a result.

nose is a small boat with its Tau-sign masts (see chapter 12, pp. 97-99 and figures 56, 57, 155, 156 and 108 in Bach, 1990). There is at least one face with a rather pathetic expression in the boat. Could this be Charon's boat and thus consistent with the imagery of death?

There is an alternative view about what this shape represents; namely a picador's hat (Baer, pers. comm.). Just touching the underside of the boat is a triangular shape which contains two eyes and a toothy mouth, amongst other shapes. Another decorated triangle connects this triangular head-shape to the body and leg of the figure riding the horse. The triangular body – either cubist or child-like – passes behind the horse's neck. Thus the picador, who has plunged his lance into the bull is doubly connected to death, since the hat apparently becomes Charon's boat.

Returning to the impact of the main images, the furious bull, the extraordinary, panic-stricken horse and the two women with their contrast of death-agony and serene calm, it seems fair to say that we have a stark portrayal of what it feels like to suffer a loss of soul, derealisation and loss of anima (see Hillman, p. 105). It is said that Picasso felt this period leading up to divorce had been the worst of his life (see Baer, 1997, p. 41).

Dionysos emerging?

Beginning in June 1933 (state 1) and finishing by the end of 1934 (state 4), Picasso produced *Marie-Thérèse Dreaming of Metamorphosis*, which therefore overlaps the production of *The Great Corrida with Female Matador*. In its first state (see Figure 7.2) we seem to be viewing a relatively uncomplicated Dionysian scene. A bearded and garlanded man, apparently unclothed, toasts a minotaur over a garlanded woman lying on her side. Mythologically, Dionysos is present not so much as the bull-god, but as the god of wine. Whereas he had affected people through the power of raw, animal emotion, he now introduces a religious element to the emotional experience of drinking (Fierz-David, 1988, p. 25). The woman's expression suggests a somewhat abstracted contentment. Perhaps she is seen rather as an object than a participant, for she has no wine-glass. The look in her eyes is somewhat sleepy and perhaps post-coital.

In the final state reproduced as Figure 7.3, two figures have been added and the drawing has become much more finely detailed (see the eyes and heads) and, at the same time, strong, dark lines are vigorously worked into the background. The minotaur's head is relatively lightly drawn, whilst the human head is more worked. Is something emerging from the underworld? It has been suggested that this minotaur is more human than others, since his tail is attached to a belt, rather than directly to his body, as in the previous state. It has been further suggested that he is balancing a minotaur's mask on his human head with his hand (Baer, 1997).

What emerges if we try to follow the lines – to see what is there, as Susan Bach would always

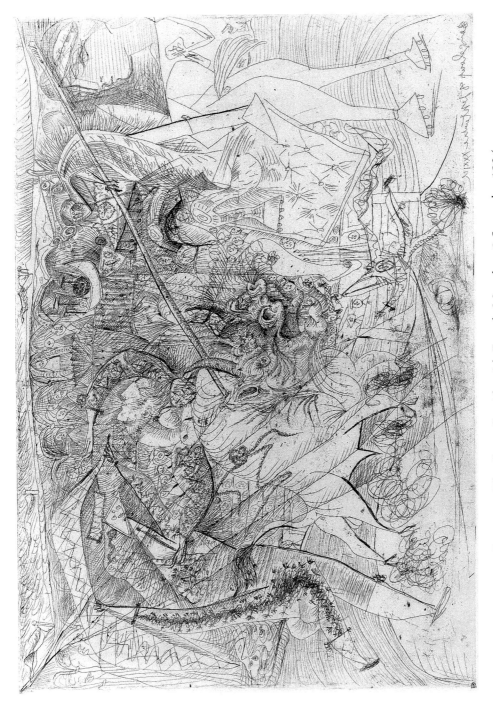

Figure 7.1 The Great Corrida with Female Matador, 8 September 1934,
Etching on copper, 497mm x 697mm, © Succession Picasso/DACS 1998

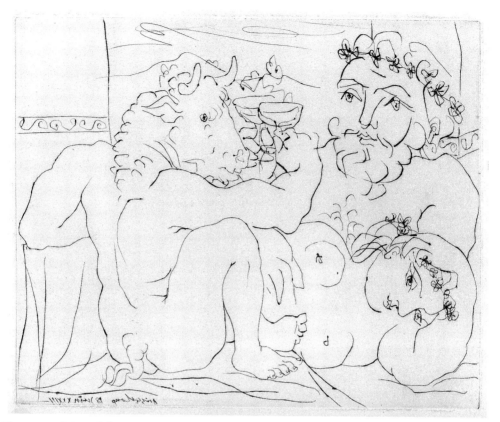

Figure 7.2 Marie-Thérèse Dreaming of Metamorphosis, *State 1, 18 June 1933, drypoint, etching, scraper and burin on copper, 298 x 365mm, © Succession Picasso/DACS 1998*

have reminded us? Then the newly added figure on the left, whose left foot is no longer visible, has lost his wine glass. Yet, via his minotaur's mask, he appears to contemplate the woman, who seems to emerge from his loins. Her gaze seems to distance her from the other players in the scene and she seems more alert and thoughtful, and has acquired the distinctive nose of Marie-Thérèse. Behind her, the satyr-like figure now has worry-lines and he has aged. His expression is serious and thoughtful. In his right hand he holds a cup or chalice directly beneath the striking eye of a woman, whose head has now appeared in the background. The shading suggests that the cup is running over, down his arm. Is this chalice the cup of redemption?

Does the underworld figure of the minotaur give birth simultaneously to a platonic form of young (androgynous) man and a newly mature Marie-Thérèse? Perhaps what is depicted, frozen in a moment, is the process of metamorphosis from the unconscious, chthonic form of Dionysian being to a humanised form. To put it another way, if the young, androgynous figure

Figure 7.3 Marie-Thérèse Dreaming of Metamorphosis, *State 4, end of 1934, drypoint, etching, scraper and burin on copper, 298 x 365mm, © Succession Picasso/DACS 1998*

is indeed removing the mask, could it be that there is a withdrawal from the world of the minotaur towards acceptance of the human psyche? The minotaur is still connected, visually-speaking, to the fleshly woman, but the androgynous, i.e. sexless figure, looks in a more outward direction with large, soulful eyes. One senses an access of consciousness, of animus in the emerging, partially masculine, person.

The composed and thoughtful-looking woman with her eye poised above the cup watches, or even provides some of the motive force for transformation: a true soul-figure doing the work of anima, rather than merely providing erotic enjoyment for the minotaur. In this final state of the etching, the woman's hands are gently resting on his upper arms, as if she is protecting and guiding the satyr. She could be a new muse replacing Marie-Thérèse, who looks out in a detached manner from the scene, as if she may be looking out towards a different and more spiritual world.

Figure 7.4 Blind Minotaur in the Starry Night 3, *7 to 31 December 1934, acquatint, scraper, drypoint and burin on copper, 246 x 348mm, © Succession Picasso/DACS 1998*

The Blind Minotaur

In many ways this is a deeply puzzling series of some seven etchings, culminating in the *Minotauromachie*. Unlike *The Great Corrida with Female Matador* and *Minotauromachie* itself, the figures are human in form, except for a Minotaur in great distress who leans on, or is led by, a child-like figure holding a dove. The child has the distinctive facial features of Marie-Thérèse. Another puzzle is the apparent doubling of the figures. There are no horses or bulls. We will discuss one print here; *Blind Minotaur in the Starry Night*. This engraving is reproduced as Figure 7.4.

Formally, this is a beautiful image of contrasted light and shade. Indeed, the dove itself seems to be the source of the light in the picture and it illuminates the ventral side of the minotaur and even the matelot's jersey in the boat.

The issues of composition of the figures in this series were clearly important and the number of the figures stays almost unchanged in the Vollard suite (Picasso, 1956) series from V. 94 to V. 97 (*Blind Minotaur in the Starry Night*). The types of the figures, however, undergo some interesting transformations; for example, in the first etching, which shares the plate with an apparently unrelated etching, often referred to as the Death of Marat,[1] there is a difference of type in the portrayal of the figure on the left. Here it is clearly a young boy in matelot's clothing. Subsequently, this figure appears seated, with the familiar profile of Marie-Thérèse with a beret and matelot's clothing. In the final version, as illustrated here, Picasso returns to the portrayal of the figure as a young boy in sailor's clothes thus balancing the bearded figure in the boat, a fishing boat rather like the accepted idea of St. Peter's. Baer (*op. cit.* p. 40) suggested that this is an aspect of Picasso himself.

The emotional power seems to emanate from the drawing of the minotaur; particularly his rigid stance, arched head and open mouth. This figure stands in contrast to the relative impassivity of the others. The left-most version of Marie-Thérèse is thoughtful, with a finger held to her lip, but undisturbed. The smaller girl with dove, whose wings are beginning to spread, is also calm, but intent. The same may be said for the fishermen, except that the lower one is looking out at the viewer. Strikingly, his hands become one with the fishing net.

The minotaur is on the shore; he is not a figure from the deep, but the net is cast in his direction. Water is a symbol of the unknown, the unconscious, and fish may be said to represent the contents of the unconscious, being the contents of the water (Jung *et al*, 1964). Christ entrusted Peter with the role of Fisher of Souls and the Dove is commonly a symbol of the Holy Spirit. The Dove may be associated with annunciation; for example, Poussin's *Annunciation*. According to Cooper (1979), it may also be associated with the idea of soul passing from one state or world to another and even the waters of creation. Yet here Marie-Thérèse clutches the Dove to her and seems to clip its wings, as it were; to inhibit its passage to another state. In terms of Picasso's biography, we can ask if Picasso is regretting his ties to Marie-Thérèse and struggling with the psychological hold her image has over him?

At the bottom left hand side, there may be three entwined fishes which would portray the Trinity (Cooper, 1979). Fishes depicted with birds are chthonic and funerary and represent hope of resurrection, as well as being a familiar symbol of early Christianity. It is equally possible to see these entwined objects as (sea-)snakes and, if so, they provide a way back to

---

[1] Once again it seems that ascribed titles can mislead later students. Viewed in the original, we can see the characteristic profile of Marie-Thérèse being stabbed by a figure with a face, whose style is very familiar and may be a reflection of Picasso's feelings about Olga. The face has a wide-open mouth with small, stabbing teeth. This image was much used by Picasso in full-scale paintings such as *Grand Nu au Fauteuil rouge* 1931 and *Woman Writing a Letter,* January, 1932. Both are in the Musée Picasso, Paris.

Dionysos. As Fierz-David (1988, p. 36-40) made clear, the symbolism of the snake extended to a hidden, healing wisdom which came as an ancestral secret from the dark night. The Thracian Dionysos, as ruler of the dead and of souls, had the same meaning. But the snake has the power to cause great turmoil and anxiety, symbolically and actually. Great emotion is an almost inevitable companion and motivator of change.

Therefore, there is a direct and urgent question; can this partly instinctive, unconscious and underworld being, the minotaur, be redeemed and acquire a human soul? Is this a picture of the redemptive possibilities of the anima-animus syzygy, the soul-maker?

We may now understand the doubling of the figures as twinned images operating at two different levels[1]; a more down-to-earth human and personal representation and a more spiritual, imaginal and archetypal representation. Thus, the earthly versions are drawn much larger and are more literal and more three-dimensional. Marie-Thérèse is present in a detached and rather boyish form, lacking the erotic charge that inspired Picasso's art hitherto. The more human matelot works on the sail, whilst the other is engaged on altogether more mysterious work. And most mysterious is the girl with dove, who appears to lead the distraught minotaur, desperately clutching his staff.

On the personal level the appearance of the Dove as an announcer, or messenger, is tantalising, for it is possible that Picasso and Marie-Thérèse knew she was pregnant by then. This question will be examined further in the next section.

The Minotauromachie

This enormous etching is virtually the same size as *The Great Corrida with Female Matador* at 494 x 687 mm. It is reproduced here in its sixth state as Figure 7.5. From its first state (see Baer, p. 77, *op. cit.*), there is a clear dividing line across the centre from top to bottom and all the figures are in place. It is already raining, but there is no differential shading and lightening of different areas or figures. As the engraving progresses through seven states, it really becomes a process of refining the light and the dark: a suspension of life between two states, or of life in the middle of a transition.

In terms of formal properties, we note the flattened perspective under the horse and the legs of the matador, which emphasises the central figures. The left foreleg of the horse and the legs of the matador form an elegant parallelogram, consistent with other rectilinear features of the drawing, which contrast with the matador's curves. The sword and the minotaur taken together form three sides of a square and continue the vertical line of the wall. Studying the originals, it is apparent that the girl with the light is looking at the matador's face. The line of

---

[1] See the chapter by Dr. Brutsche for a discussion of a dream depicting two different kinds of relationships [Editor].

Figure 7.5 Minotauromachie, 23 March-3 May 1935, state 6, etching, scraper and burin on copper, 494mm x 687mm, © Succession Picasso/DACS 1998

the shoulder of the man on the ladder, parallel to the right foreleg of the horse, can be continued to the matador's heart, between her breasts.

Concentrating on the female matador, she seems either dead or asleep across the horse – her expression with mouth closed is very peaceful, even content, as depicted in the original *Death of the Female Torera*, mentioned on page 87. She is dark to the left side and her upper torso is light. The upraised arm of the enormous minotaur passes from the light to the dark side, across the sharp vertical division, or wall. The minotaur carries a huge, dark sack, outlined against a lighter, but lowering sky. The horse is a light (white) figure, as is the young girl with flowers and a lighted candle. The paradoxical male figure, precariously balanced on the ladder, is light in contrast to the dark head of the minotaur. There is a fair-haired girl with a dark-haired girl, heads inclined towards each other, in the alcove with a light and a dark dove. The darker dove (on the right) appears to be hooded with a dark, mask-like shape around the eyes. There is also a dish on the ledge in front of the two birds. A little boat, sail set, is skimming across the waves, pointing towards shore.

Having sketched the wider view, let us focus on the figures, which seem again to be doubled, or twinned. Across the centre is the female matador[1], p. 58, with her very full breasts and rise of her belly revealed. Her breasts directly recall those of the female matador across the back of the bull in *The Great Corrida with Female Matador* and if we look carefully, examining the line and the shading, we can see that she too is pregnant. As far as we are aware, no art historians have made this observation and we will comment further below. Between her breasts, forming an elaborate, erotic diamond, is drawn the torn fabric of her dress shirt.

The head has the same profile as that of the girl holding the candle; again we seem to be presented with two sides of Marie-Thérèse. The spiritual and virginal girl with curly hair (or her hair done in ringlets, echoing the mane of the horse as part of the circle of light) offering flowers – Blunt (*op. cit.*) writes of the light of truth and innocence – and the concupiscent woman. However, the candle may also have a negative side, for the minotaur seems to be trying to occlude it with a great hand or paw; a kind of bestial arm compared with his human left hand across his heart. Is the innocent girl really a temptress trying to return the minotaur to the underworld? Here the male aspect of the twinning is relevant, for we have the figure whose feet scarcely touch the ladder. Is he climbing up or down? Commonly, according to Blunt (*op. cit.*), we can take such figures to be Picasso himself and, if so, he is clearly in poor case. He has a Greek hero's head as in *The Sculptor's Studio* series in the Vollard suite (*op. cit.*), but the body of a weak and indecisive man. At least the minotaur, although burdened by his sack, is still a powerful and sure-footed beast. In earlier states (e.g. state 2), the bearded man's mouth is quite wide open, as if expressing a degree of shock.

---

[1] To our surprise, female matadors were not completely unknown, even in the 1930s. See Pink on "Breasts in the Bullring ..." (Pink, 1996)

Alternatively, or additionally, it could be said that the light of the candle falls on the horse and the matador's body and face. Is Marie-Thérèse in her virginal innocence, dressed for Church, contemplating her downfall and pregnancy? When Mary heard the words of Simeon (at Jesus' circumcision) she knew that her soul would be pierced as by a sword (see Luke, ch. 2, vv. 34-35). The figure across the horse holds a sword pointing directly away from the minotaur and towards the horse and the hands of the matador and the minotaur are just touching.

The horse is half black and half white and hairy like the minotaur and the bull. The horse is sacrificed as usual in the bullfight etchings and as so often in the Corrida, for here its entrails pour onto the ground. Yet the horse has an innocent, even stupid look, and appears unaware of pain, as it faces the sword. Even the earth nourished by the horse's entrails becomes "pregnant" in accord with the old legends of a bull's blood nurturing the earth! (See page 88) Furthermore, the curve of the ground echoes the curve of Marie-Thérèse's belly.

The direction of the ritual sword (the *espada*) emphasises the fact that the horse is in its death throes, even as the pregnancy of the *torera* develops. Death and birth as transformation are a significant part of what we are witnessing in this engraving; specifically, the feminine instinctive side, represented by the horse and the young, erotic *torera* are giving way to another level, to the mother-figure, or Madonna. The pregnant torera is in the process of metamorphosing (figuratively dying) into a mother.

Thus, in this engraving we have a "fallen woman", one who has fallen pregnant, and a pure young girl dressed for Church. On one side these figures are framed by the helpless Christ-like figure and on the other by the menacing minotaur. The torera, who is the fallen woman, is linked pictorially with the minotaur, whereas the innocent girl, above whom the white dove sits, is spatially linked to the Christ-like figure. It is worth noting that it was only in the third state of the engraving that the girl was given a hat and therefore dressed for Church. The minotaur and the torera are unmistakably sexual, with lovingly drawn, idealised bodies. The figure on the ladder and the girl share an almost inept-looking childishness and lack of corporeality. In state 2, Marie-Thérèse has emerging, pubescent breasts, which have been quite definitely shaded over with horizontal strokes to flatten her chest and thereby emphasise her prepubertal, asexual nature in later states.

Fierz-David (*ibid.*) discussed the possibility that, in the second scene of the Villa Mystery in Pompeii, the woman is apparently pregnant (p. 36). More specifically, that something has penetrated her and arrived in her bowels, which is nevertheless insubstantial. In turn, this observation may be connected with the cult of the Phrygian Dionysos, wherein a snake was pulled through the garment of the participant in the mystery. In this rite, Dionysos was referred to as the god who goes through the bosom. "To take into the bosom" was a Greek expression for conception. It seems that the disparate mythic roots converge on a common symbolism of recreation and rebirth; in short, of transformation.

Returning to biographical facts (see p. 86), we note that Marie-Thérèse would have been approximately four and a half months pregnant at the time of the early states of the

Minotauromachie. If we count the rungs of the ladder, we find four and a half are visible, when there is space for nine. The importance of counting objects has been repeatedly demonstrated by Susan Bach; the direct comparison here is with her chapter 12, the Motif of the Ladder.[1]

Meanwhile the minotaur wears more of a benign rather than threatening expression and posture; the figure is nearly all light except for the menacing arm thrusting to the right, as already described. The arm looks evil and rapacious as if trying to put out the light, not reaching towards it. This implies that the minotaur is not blind, for he can establish where the light is. He can see, but he is not looking, like so many of us! He has created chaos, but he is not looking where he is going; he looks out at us innocently in an echo of the horse's stupid innocence. There is no real fear. Does the minotaur also have the role of a narrator as in Greek tragedy? He looks out at the viewer like the bull in *Guernica*. His horns are asymmetric (unlike any good fighting bull) and the more twisted one is on the same side as the threatening arm, which incidentally corresponds to the right foot. Is the minotaur weakened and submissive, perhaps in a decaying state? Not unlike the uncertain, even precarious state of the man on the ladder. We have already noted that it is unusual for Picasso to represent the horse as male, and Chipp (*ibid.*, p. 52), among others, has noted that the bull usually represents the masculine element and the horse the feminine. The horse occupies such a central position that we are compelled to attend to it, although viewers are often disturbed and distracted by the minotaur. Thus, by drawing out the symbolism of the horse we have completed our understanding of all the major protagonists, who have appeared so often in the works of Picasso. In this sense, we agree with Baer who suggested (pers. comm. and see p. 40 of Baer, 1997) that the actors were taking their last bow in *Minotauromachie*.

There are two pairs of minor protagonists, the two women and two doves in the alcove, which have puzzled many writers. Doves have already appeared in this series of engravings, especially in the blind minotaur series, one engraving of which we have already discussed above. We note that both doves are looking at the figure on the ladder, whilst the two women are looking down at the central action. Once more there is a form of doubling; the doves are more obviously symbolic than the women. Doves drinking from a bowl depict the Spirit drinking the waters of life (Cooper, 1979, p. 54) and here the doves' gaze is directed towards the man on the ladder, who may be a symbol of Christ as already described. In this context, what can we say of the two women? They are important in the composition, but in the state reproduced here the women are at their most poorly defined. They seem to be spectators of the action and so may represent more individual persons, or more muse-like, anima figures. Other writers have speculated that the dark-haired woman is Marie-Thérèse's sister (with whom Marie-Thérèse was close; see Gedo, 1980, p. 161) and that the fair-haired woman is Marie-Thérèse, but she is already well represented here! The doubling of dark and light parallels the role of the

---

[1] See also *The Viking Ship* picture (Figure 2.5) in Dr. Kiepenheuer's chapter concerning the child with leukaemia [Editor].

two women in the main action below, the fallen woman and the girl holding the light. They are therefore closer to persons than symbols, but without a specific identity – a common occurrence in dreams.

Taken overall the mood is one of sacrifice. Picasso has two sides; a hairy, bull-like, sexually bacchanalian side and the spiritual, human side of one who feels deeply and wants to cherish and protect the mother of his child. (And Picasso did indeed cherish Maya and spend time with her and with Marie-Thérèse after the birth.) Therefore, we may see the need to portray a theriomorphic form, or chimaera. The problem to be solved seems to be one of *reconciliation*, through sacrifice, of the lustfully generative compared to the loving acceptance of parenthood, and, secondly, the creative in the sense of art and spirit compared to the Dionysian. Here too is the tension between the light and dark anima. So much for the masculine side of the picture.

In general, one can say that there are two routes to becoming a mother / Madonna. One route is to travel from virginal and innocent girl through the transformative ceremonies of the Church or other religious institution within a society, to wife and hence mother. The alternative route is to pass from girlhood into a period of living an instinctive life, which is transformed by pregnancy and without benefit of public ceremony or ritual. These two possibilities seem to be represented in *Minotauromachie*, since Marie-Thérèse moved from girlhood via the instinctive *torera* to motherhood. These routes, or vectors[1], have no direct masculine parallel.

Towards a Resolution

Hillman (*op. cit.* p. 75) points out that Jung associates a host of feminine forms with anima; but one in particular he generally keeps outside its confines. It is that of the mother. "The most striking feature about the anima-type is that the maternal element is lacking." This is a direct reminder of Hans Bach's findings quoted on page 88, concerning Dionysos. Whilst he is the god of the phallus, he is not worshipped as the source of procreation, nor mentioned in relation to marriage or family. Furthermore, we have seen an identification, at least in part, between Picasso and the form of the minotaur and bull, thus reaching back to the ancient legend. Therefore, we should look most carefully at what happens to Picasso, biographically, when Marie-Thérèse moves from anima figure to actual mother / Madonna.

Chipp (*op. cit.* p. 62) makes the point very clearly that Picasso's attitude to Marie-Thérèse changed after the birth of Maya and that this is reflected in his paintings and drawings of Marie-Thérèse.

---

[1] We are indebted to Dr. Ian Pennell, Newtown Hospital, Worcester, for this suggestion.

This suggests a new way to think about *Minotauromachie* and the other engravings we have described. Perhaps they represent the process of escape from the Shadow and the associated Dionysian underworld, linked to domination by an erotic, albeit muse-like, anima figure. In the *Minotauromachie*, Marie-Thérèse is transformed into a spiritual anima-figure, bearing a powerful light, which she shines in the minotaur's face. It seems to be an almost unbearable light of consciousness. Yet the Minotaur / Picasso pair know that transformation, or redemption, is necessary to life, for only then is it possible to embrace middle age, to make new relationships and to renew creativity in the shape of *Guernica*, 1937. One of the important aspects of *Guernica* is that so much of the iconography had gone before and yet could now serve to raise a painting to the level of the sacral, as Neumann described it. (See also chapter five of Chipp, 1988.)

This suggestion is closely paralleled by Seckel (1973) in his later paper. He concluded:

The path through a symbolic exploration has changed his personal fate into one of archetypal universality and has at the same time made it possible for him to find release from his own chaotic feelings through working on a picture of the highest artistic quality.

(Translated by Brigitte Kay)

Conclusion

We have tried to show four things; firstly, that a systematic way of looking learnt from Susan Bach's research can be helpful when looking at works of art. Secondly, we have described reasons deduced from both form and symbol to suggest that Picasso's Minotaur series both illuminates, and is illuminated by, the notions of animus and anima and, indeed that they may be part of the same discourse[1]. Thirdly, we have proposed that the apparent pregnancies in two of these pictures (especially *Minotauromachie*) are central to a more complete understanding of these pictures. Fourthly, we conclude that Jung's initial attempt to illuminate Picasso's work from a psychological point of view, using the notion of the light and dark anima, continues to be fruitful, especially when allied to the notions of personification and amplification.

Acknowledgement

We are very grateful to the *Musée Picasso* in Paris for their great courtesy and helpfulness in enabling us to view these engravings. We are also grateful To Mme. B. Baer, Paris, for giving us some time for a stimulating conversation. We should emphasise that the views expressed here are ours, unless specifically attributed.

[1] We are indebted to Dr. T. O'Connor, Cheltenham College of Higher Education, for this observation.

References

Bach, H. I. (1973). On the archetypal complex: His father's son. *Quadrant*, 15:4-31.

Bach, S. R. (1969). Spontaneous paintings of severely ill patients. *Acta Psychosomatica*, 8.

Bach, S. R. (1990). *Life Paints Its Own Span: On the Significance of Spontaneous Pictures by Severely Ill Children*. Daimon.

Baer, B. (1997). *Picasso The Engraver*. Thames and Hudson, London.

Blunt, A. (1969). *Picasso's Guernica*. Oxford University Press.

Chipp, H. B. (1988). *Picasso's Guernica: History, Transformations, Meanings*. Thames and Hudson, London.

Cooper, J. (1979). *An Illustrated Encyclopaedia of Traditional Symbols*. Thames and Hudson.

Fierz-David, L. (1988). *Women's Dionysian Initiation: The Villa Mysteries in Pompeii*. Spring Publications, Texas.

Gedo, M. M. (1980). *Picasso: Art as Autobiography*. University of Chicago Press, London.

Hillman, J. (1985). *Anima: An Anatomy of a Personified Notion*. Spring Publications, USA.

Jung, C.G. et al (1964). *Man and his Symbols*. Picador.

Jung, C.G. (1966/1984). *The Spirit in Man, Art and Literature*. ARK.

Neumann, E. (1959). *Art and the Creative Unconscious*. Routledge and Kegan Paul.

O'Brian, P. (1976). *Pablo Ruiz Picasso: A Biography*. Collins, London.

Picasso, P. (1956). *Picasso's Vollard Suite*. Thames and Hudson, London.

Pink, S. (1996). Breasts in the bullring: Female physiology, female bullfighters and competing femininities. *Body and Society*, 2:45-64.

Seckel, C. (1959). Die Minotauromachie: Bildhafte Meditation aus einem Schicksalsjahr Picassos. *Zeitwende: Die Neue Furche*, 30 Jahrgang: 245-251.

Seckel, C. (1973). Picassos Wege zur Symbolik der Minotauromachie. *Die Kunst und das Schöne Heim*, 85 Jahrgang.

Ulanov, A. and B. Ulanov (1994). *Transforming Sexuality: The Archetypal World of Anima and Animus*. Shambhala, London.

The Inner Figure: Synchronistic Images of the Soul

by Cedrus Monte

Introduction

The Inner Figure is a process that involves making a figure of clay and other materials which forms itself around a numinous, or archetypal experience. It is a course in active imagination which I developed out of studying ritual doll-making, ritual theatre, and Jungian psychology.[1]

The main focus of this discussion is to illustrate how synchronistic phenomena are related to the imaginal realm and the process of image-making. I use the *The Inner Figure*, a nine-month long class which I have taught since 1983, as the primary example for the image-making process. At the conclusion of the discussion are two individual stories from *The Inner Figure* course, demonstrating the unique nature of the synchronistic events which form around the making of a figure. The first story is about "Regina", one of the participants in *The Inner Figure* course. The second story is my own. In each class I make my own figure.

The Imaginal Realm

> *The soul never thinks without a picture.*
> – Aristotle

C. G. Jung's formulation of the unconscious, primarily the collective unconscious, is important to note because it lays the groundwork for the retrieval of the mythical, imaginal

[1] The research for writing *The Inner Figure: Synchronistic Images of the Soul* was conducted under the auspices of a grant from The Susan Bach Foundation, and was formulated as Cedrus Monte's thesis for her diploma in analytical psychology from the C.G. Jung Institute in Zürich (1997). This article is an extensively abridged version of the more complete study written under the same title.

world view. One could say that Jung returned the soul back to the psyche, primarily through his psychologically vivifying relationship to the unconscious, and to the mythicalizing voice of imagination and image by which it speaks. Jung liberated a whole dimension of human experience or understanding for the non-indigenous Western world by honouring the ubiquitous, *a priori* image-making capacity of humankind. According to Jung, "Every psychic process is an image and an imagining" (CW 6, § 77).

Jung was one of the forerunners in redeeming the imaginal world for 20th-century Western civilization. As such, he helped redeem a well-spring from which life regenerates itself. Imaginal, mythical time is the time in which the origins of life are held. If we consider creation myths in particular, we see that they are universally used to restore and revivify. In Fiji, for example, when feeling something is out of balance, or that life is threatened, or the cosmos, in their view, is exhausted or empty, the Fijians return to the beginning of time, *in principio*, to mythological time, seeking a restored sense of life from its ritual re-creation. "Whenever they are threatened by dissociation and panic and social disorder, they try to restore the creation and the whole cosmos by retelling the creation myth. They create again, as it were, the conscious order of things and then await the corresponding effect upon their souls, which would mean that they once again feel themselves to be in order" (von Franz 1972/95, p. 23).

The phenomenon of imaginal reality presents itself quite pointedly in the writings of Western alchemy which inspired much of Jung's later formulations on the nature of the psyche. Jung explains that the term *imaginatio* held particular importance in the opus of the alchemists who believed that "the work" must be accomplished with "true imagination". Jung felt that the fantasy process in alchemy, whereby images of figures were seen in the retort, was of special significance. The imaginal phenomena referred to by the alchemists were "half spiritual, half physical …. The alchemist related himself not only to the unconscious but directly to the very substance which he hoped to transform through the power of the imagination" (CW 12, § 394). The imaginings were "an intermediate realm between mind and matter, i.e., a psychic realm of subtle bodies whose characteristic is to manifest themselves in a mental as well as material form" (*ibid.*). We see this notion, for example, in the writings of alchemist Raymond Lilly when he says:

> You should know, dear son, that the course of nature is turned about so that without invocation … and without spiritual exaltation you can see certain fugitive spirits condensed in the air in the shape of divers monsters, beasts and men, which move like the clouds hither and thither. (*ibid.*, § 351)

Jung found repeated reference to the necessity of imagination in the alchemists' writings. One particularly striking statement invokes the following claim:

> Imagination is the star in man, the celestial or super-celestial body. (*ibid.*, § 394)

"Star" in this case was understood or translated as the "quintessence" of humankind. Imagination, then, according to the alchemists, is the "quintessence", or essence, of us. Imagination, our essence, is the subtle-body state of material and spiritual equivalence. Particle and wave are one.

As I will explain more fully later, it is from the ground of the imaginal realm – the subtle-body dimension of matter as spirit, and spirit as matter – that synchronistic experiences arise. From the synchronistic follows the transformative power of the numen: the healing, regenerative shock from contact with the Divine.

In addition to entering mythical, imaginal time through the ritual re-enactment of creation myths and the alchemical opus, the imaginal realm can be accessed through the conscious making of images that arise from the unconscious. I offer *The Inner Figure* as a possible, contemporary example of an imaginative process where life can be potentially recreated, regenerated through the subtle-body world of the synchronistic event.

The Inner Figure

To give both psychological and historical background to our discussion of *The Inner Figure*, we will begin with a fairy tale, followed by other cross-cultural references to dolls or figures.

In Russia, a story is told by the name of *Vasalisa*. It is an initiation story, the initiation into one's intuition. Sometimes the story is called *Wassalissa the Wise*, or *The Doll* (Estés 1992, p. 75). The story tells us about a young girl whose mother has passed away. Before her mother dies, however, she leaves her daughter a tiny doll, saying, "Here are my last words, Beloved. Should you lose your way or be in need of help, ask this doll what to do. You will be assisted. Keep the doll with you always." The story continues with Vasalisa's father remarrying and bringing home two malcontent step-daughters along with his new and equally ungracious wife. These newcomers mistreat Vasalisa terribly, reducing her to the kitchen slave, all the while being terribly jealous of her beauty and goodness. Finally, out of the sheer exasperation and frustration of their own envy, they send her away. They conspire to let the fire in the house go out and enlist Vasalisa as the volunteer to go deep into the forest to retrieve fire from Baba Yaga, fierce and terrifying guardian of the flame. Little Vasalisa dutifully agrees to go. The three women believe this is her doom and that she will never return, to be eaten as dessert by the Baba Yaga.

Vasalisa sets out, doll in pocket. As she progresses deeper into the forest she asks the doll to help guide her through the dark wood. She reaches into her pocket each time a question arises: "Left or right?" "This way or that?" As her dying mother promised, the doll indicates the way. Vasalisa feeds the doll some bread from time to time and follows the impulses she feels coming from the doll. Finally, she reaches the house of Baba Yaga. Standing at the front gate she consults the doll who confirms that this is indeed the place. She has arrived.

Vasalisa stands in front of the Baba Yaga and humbly asks for fire to save the life of her people, her family. The Baba Yaga is not at all inclined simply to hand over a portion of the burning light unconditionally: Vasalisa must perform a few seemingly impossible tasks first, and then *maybe* she will be given a piece of the flame. She must separate mildewed corn from good corn, dirt from poppy seeds, and do endless lists of things before morning. With the help and guidance of her doll she is able to complete each and every task. She is even able to answer the questions put to her by the Baba Yaga. No easy feat with this Old Hag. But it is the instructions given to her by the doll – jumping in her pocket this way, moving at just the right moment that way – that guide her to the successful completion of her tasks. And so she receives the flame from the Baba Yaga, which is put in one of the skulls decorating Baba Yaga's fence, and is sent on her way. She runs for home, with the doll helping the whole while. Approaching her house, the step-mother and step-daughters rush out to meet her, saying that they had been without fire the entire time, for no matter how hard they tried they could spark not one flame. That night, as the step-mother and the step-sisters sleep, the skull stares at them relentlessly. In the morning, The Ugly Three are found, justifiably burnt to cinders (*ibid.*, p. 75-80).

According to Estés, Vasalisa is a tale of a woman's initiation to the ways of The Wise One, *La Que Sabé*, The One Who Knows (*ibid.*, p. 74). By listening to the messages of the doll, she reaches the Baba Yaga and successfully completes all that is required. The flame is then passed on to her. By learning to trust and follow our intuition, we are initiated into our own reserves of inner knowing, we learn how to tap into the unconscious and move toward making what is unconscious conscious. We become street-wise as we follow the road map of intuitive signals. By listening to the doll and by feeding it, Vasalisa is navigated successfully through the dark of the deep forest, back to her home and on to a life transformed, without the presence of The Three Ugly Ones.

The role of the doll as it appears in *Vasalisa*, as the impulse or vortex of our intuition or inner voice, is directly related to The Inner Figure. But before going more deeply into *The Inner Figure* as an access to intuition, to our inner knowing, I would like to describe other related aspects in the symbolism of the doll or figure to show the wide range that this symbol encompasses, and to illustrate its cross-cultural dimensions.

In different cultures and at different times in history, the figure or doll has been the object of considerable numinosity. From religious icons to the black magic dolls of voodoo, these figures have been seen as the receptor for projections, on the one hand; and for visitations from the gods, on the other. Dolls carry these projections, this life-force infused into them, and are believed then to emanate this vivification. As in the tale of *Vasalisa*, they are able to affect the people and time of their environment. In this sense they are carriers for "energy", receiving and emanating life-force or mana.

Japanese culture is highly punctuated with doll traditions. In fact, one of the highest art forms in Japan is the art of puppet theatre known as *Bunraku*. Although puppet and doll traditions of Japan date much earlier, *Bunraku* first appeared in the early sixteenth century. The older doll traditions are connected with religious worship at particular Shinto shrines.

> Puppets preserved today at shrines in scattered areas of Japan clearly suggest ancient traditions behind them. In the north, the worship of the god Oshira involves a medium who recites spells and stories accompanied by the two simple stick puppets she operates, one in each hand, raising, lowering, or confronting the puppets as she speaks …. These Shinto puppets are not representations of divinities … but, rather, wooden creatures temporarily "possessed" by the gods they recreate, much as the medium herself is believed to repeat, when "possessed", words uttered by the god himself. Puppet performances at a shrine are intended to depict deeds of the ancient past in order that men of later ages may know the glory of the divinity worshipped there. (Keene 1965, p. 19.)

In churches throughout the world one sees the presence of dolls or figures in statue form. These statues are very carefully tended, often wearing opulent, handmade clothing. They are given a special place of their own in the church where people can come and offer their prayers to the presence that is guarded by and radiates from the figure or statue. These figures are often bathed at different times of the year and are also sometimes taken out of their everyday residence and brought out into the community "so they might see the conditions of the fields and of the people, and therefore intercede with heaven in the human's behalf" (Estés 1992, p. 88). The Black Madonna at Einsiedeln Monastery in Switzerland is one prominent example of this type of figure. The icons of Russia also have this status, with special times of the year being marked by the procession of the icons into the towns and villages where they reside.

In this regard, the statue, doll, or figure "is the symbol of what lies buried in humans that is numinous. It is a small and glowing facsimile of the original Self. Superficially it is just a doll. But inversely, there is a little piece of soul that carries all the knowledge of the larger soul-Self. In this way the doll represents the inner spirit … the voice of inner reason, inner knowing, and inner consciousness" (*ibid.*, p. 88). And because of this the doll, or figure, can intercede on our behalf; it is a vortex through which spirit and matter are inter-related.

As we shall see below, *The Inner Figure* process consciously allows for the voice of inner knowing and inner consciousness to present itself to the image-maker.

The Inner Figure Process

The figures made in this course arise out of a process known in Jungian psychology as active imagination. This process can also be seen as a form of ritual image-making. Whichever perspective one takes – Jungian, ritualistic or otherwise – in working with the figures, one is working with the evocation of the inner voice in image form. Through the meditative act of making *The Inner Figure* one constellates a mirror of the soul.

Approximately nine months of story, prayer, and envisioning go into each of the figures, which are both vessel and mirror for these experiences. They are both magnet and transmitter for the energy that they invoke and embody. Each figure is a dream in concrete form, a living symbol for the maker of the figure. Years after the figures are completed they can continue to tell their story, much as a dream continues to teach us of ourselves long after it is dreamt.

At each weekly session of the course, the evening is divided into two parts. In the second two hours the actual figure itself is formed. The first part of the evening starts with a simple meditation and ritual where the boundary between the secular world and the sacred or numinous world is drawn. The everyday world is suspended just long enough to recognize, acknowledge and invite the presence of the inner voice: The imaginal realm is activated, the symbols of our individual lives are given time and space to step forward, the personal and collective unconscious offers up the images needing a body. As Vasalisa fed her doll bread, it is during this time that we feed our intuition. Through various forms of meditation, participants are led to different inner characters or images upon which to reflect, or who actually communicate something in word or deed. Sometimes an animal appears and offers something; or a childhood memory is recalled; a new person is met and spoken with; or one has a dream-like experience. As in Vasalisa's story, all these are occasions of the doll jumping up and down in our pockets saying, "This way!" "Now that way!" Guiding us on our journey. These experiences are also the nature, the essence, of the figure itself being revealed to us. And the essence of the figure is the quintessential image or message of our intuition which we are building, making, activating, in order to understand what the inner voice wants us to know. Through the doll, or *The Inner Figure*, we are making our dream, living our dream more fully. We are coming awake to it. In Jungian terms, the figure acts as a guide and catalyst in the individuation process.

Synchronicity and The Inner Figure

As previously mentioned, primary to the intention of this inquiry is to describe how *The Inner Figure* process calls forth synchronistic experiences in the lives of the figure-makers, resulting in contact with the healing of the numinous.

Speaking on synchronicity Jung writes:

As it is not limited to the person, it is also not limited to the body. It manifests itself therefore not only in human beings, but also at the same time in animals and even physical circumstances .... I call these latter phenomena the Synchronicity of archetypal events. For instance, I walk with a woman patient in a wood. She tells me about the first dream in her life that had made an everlasting impression upon her. She had seen a spectral fox coming down the stairs in her parental home. At this moment a real fox comes out of the trees not

40 yards away and walks quietly on the path ahead of us for several minutes. The animal behaves as if it were a partner in the human situation. (Letters, Vol. 1; p. 395, 1973.)

Throughout *The Inner Figure* process the world-at-large offers itself to the course participants in the form of these synchronistic, archetypal events. It is the figure itself, in all its different physical aspects, that registers and holds the events as a whole. For nine months the archetype, and therefore the synchronistic, is courted revealing to each of us, in the end, a piece of our individuation mystery.

Jung proposes that a synchronistic phenomenon consists of two parts. An unconscious content will come into consciousness as some kind of image – a dream, an idea, or a premonition. This image will then correspond to a real situation that occurs in some form, and will coincide with the image in meaning (CW 8, § 426ff). In synchronistic events, "one and the same … meaning might manifest itself simultaneously in the human psyche and in the arrangement of an external and independent event" (*ibid.*, § 482).

One of the most fundamental aspects, then, in synchronistic events, and what makes synchronicity different than two things simply happening at the same time, is the element of meaning that is constellated as a result of two seemingly disparate events coming into relationship with one another. They are not related to each other causally, but through their equivalent meaning (von Franz 1992, p. 160). Furthermore, the "'meaning' of a synchronistic phenomenon visibly participates in the nature of the 'absolute knowledge' of the unconscious…. The realization of 'meaning' is therefore not a simple acquisition of information or of knowledge, but rather *a living experience that touches the heart just as much as the mind*. It seems to us to be an illumination characterized by great clarity as well as something ineffable – a lightning flash…." (von Franz 1980, p. 257, italics mine). The experience of meaning as thus described – "a lightning flash, a living experience that touches the heart" – occurred frequently during *The Inner Figure* process. Through the participant's stories, one will observe that in the process of making *The Inner Figure*, a knowledge in the form of symbolic images breaks through, bringing past and/or future events together in and through the concrete symbol of the figure itself, and which is experienced as a sudden realization coming to consciousness.

While the components of synchronistic events are united by their common meaning, they occur *both at the level of matter and psyche*: the two levels coincide. Clinical experience led Jung to understand the archetypes underlying synchronistic events as *psychoid*, i.e., as structuring patterns for both psyche and matter. Von Franz states that it is "quite correct to say that at the moment of a synchronistic event the psyche behaves as if it were matter and matter behaves as if it belonged to an individual psyche … there is a sort of *coniunctio* of matter and psyche …. So it is really true that a synchronistic event is an act of creation and a union of two principles normally not connected" (von Franz 1980, p. 116). This liminal, psychoid state was called up again and again in the experience of the doll-course participants, and was also constellated for many people in simply observing the figures themselves for the first time. One had the feeling of entering a numinous dream, in and through the concrete object of the figure.

Because of the numinosity of the *coniunctio* of matter and psyche, because of the shock it creates to our causal thinking, it can be noted that in times past (and present) these synchronistic events have been called signs of the gods, or miracles. This numinous state of affairs always brings something new into one's life, new growth or awareness, the dimension of the Divine Child. Synchronistic events, then, tend to happen when a person is encouraged or pushed by the unconscious toward a new birth, a creative discovery or toward progress in becoming conscious (von Franz 1992, p. 160). Many of the participants entering *The Inner Figure* course were unequivocally drawn to the process, some without ever having met me before coming to the course, or having seen the figures. They had only heard about the process or the figures from others. It seems apparent to me that the Divine Child was urgently calling for its birth through this process, seeking a way to become conscious in each participant.

Synchronistic events always arise in connection with an activated archetype (CW 8, § 499). Indeed, the only factor that seems to be close to a law in the case of synchronistic phenomena is that they tend to take place when an archetype is strongly constellated in the field of the experiencer. In events that contain the archetypal – death, birth, deeply intimate relationships, life passages – that is, in all the profound events of life that humanity shares, in which the archetypal level of the unconscious is constellated, synchronistic events tend to occur (von Franz 1992, p. 27). One can see these factors clearly operative in *The Inner Figure* process when one carefully observes the evolution of each doll. Especially in cases where synchronistic events occurred quite dramatically, there was the undeniable experience of the numinous at hand, of a profound event which opened the way to further self-realization.

Outside time and outside space, the archetypes are eternal (Jung, 1952 Letters, Vol. 2, p. 46). Because, as previously noted, the archetype and the synchronistic event are directly tied, synchronistic events then are outside the causal, materialistic construct. In this eternal, timeless space we can re-create ourselves, re-address life situations, because it opens or coincides with a space in time for something new and numinous, and therefore potentially healing, to happen. Jung fostered a belief in a *creatio continua*, like certain physicists who believe that there is in the world a place where from time to time new things are created. Jung believed that synchronistic events would be such acts of creation (von Franz 1980, p. 110).

As I described above, it has been my observation that the figures repeatedly become a focal point, a magnet, for the occurrence of synchronistic phenomena, and give us an opportunity to enter the eternal, timeless space where we can re-create ourselves and re-address life situations. *The Inner Figure* process tends to ready the ground, to provide a vessel, for synchronistic occurrences, and therefore for the potentially healing, in that each figure made is virtually, almost without exception, of a numinous, archetypal nature. The archetype is invited, as it were, and therefore the synchronistic. Throughout the entire nine months of meeting each week, space is created after coming in from the everyday, secular world to engender the liminality required for contact with the unconscious, and with the archetypal realm. The burning of sacred herbs, silent meditation, guided meditation, improvisational movement, spontaneous drawings, the sharing of inner processes, and more, all contribute to the formation of an invitation to the archetype. All these activities serve to create the eternal place of the time / space continuum where something new can emerge. The physical, artistic process of making the figure rests on this ground of preparation. This time is a practice in letting the image emerge, allowing the image to take shape. From these practices the ability to listen to the inner voice is fostered. This voice comes out through the hands of the participants, making its impression through them onto the materials from which the figure is formed.

For Jung, meaning, synchronicity and individuation are intimately related. Where there is synchronicity, and therefore meaning, one also finds (with the proper understanding of the meaningful, synchronistic event) movement towards actualizing and expressing the Self's intent in our lives, a movement known as the process of individuation. In Jung's view, individuation and realization of the meaning of one's life are identical. Individuation means to find one's own meaning, which is nothing less than one's own connection with the universal Meaning. When one encounters this realization of meaning there is the experience of wholeness or unification in one's life. The sudden and illuminating experience, which one encounters with a synchronistic event, represents a momentary unification of two different psychic states: our normal state of consciousness that forms or shapes our idea of what we call the material and external world; and the state of a supra-consciousness where a profound sense of the meaning of the Whole is experienced, the sphere of absolute knowledge.

To summarize, synchronistic experiences revolve around issues of meaning, space-time transcendence, acausality, and the unity of psyche and matter. They always focus on some critical meaning closely associated with the person's individuation at that moment. As the alchemists already believed, and as quantum physics now reveals, synchronistic experiences offer us evidence that psyche and nature, or mind and matter, are not separate or disparate realms. A profound relationship or interconnection between them seems to encourage the soul to understand the same meaning in both realms. *The Inner Figure* is a vessel, alchemical or otherwise, for the synchronistic to arise and for the emergence of individual meaning. The following Inner Figure stories describe the events in this process.

Regina

> *Let yourself be drawn by the stronger pull of what you really love.*
> – Rumi

Regina originally heard about *The Inner Figure* from one of the participants who had previously taken the course. She called one evening telling me she would like to attend the nine-month-long process. This she did without ever having met me, or having seen one of the figures. She was also aware of my request that when one starts the course, one makes a commitment to finishing it. The first day of the course was the first day we met.

On the first evening of the course Regina attended, I asked everyone to draw their names in any way they chose and then to share with the group what they wished about their name and what they had drawn. Her last name is related to the English word "cellar"; and the cellar was where so many early and memorable experiences had taken place. Regina was born in Germany during the war. The bombing raids sent her and her family many times into the cellar, where she felt not only her own fear, but the fear and terror of the other members in her family who were in the cellar with her. Because of these early traumatic experiences, the cellar was equated with darkness, sadness and fear. She also remembers other unpleasant childhood experiences when she was sent to the cellar for having disobeyed or misbehaved in some way. She was a lively and active child with a fastidious and perfectionist mother whose standards of conduct were ill-suited for a frisky and tomboyish girl. She often heard, like a refrain, *"Als Mädchen macht man das nicht."* "Little girls don't do that." A stint in the cellar was her punishment. Another especially impressive and vivid childhood memory that arises from the cellar was her unquestionably real feeling of an Indian, an American Indian, waiting for her there with bow and arrow whenever she was sent to fetch beer or other items from this dark nether region. She knew he was there, and she says she could often feel the arrow shot in her back as she turned to leave.

The Cellar was a recurring and undeniably important image for Regina. From the incidents that follow, one will see how even more significant it has been in her life.

We are not required to know what figure to make before starting the process. Although one is not discouraged from making that kind of predetermination, the participants are aware that it can take time before the figure fully presents itself. In the beginning, Regina had the strong intention of making her cellar companion, the American Indian; she also felt, quite definitely, that her Indian would be a man. But after a particularly impressive experience that transpired during a movement meditation in which she encountered and 'became' *"ein Säufer, ein Landstreicher"*, "an alcoholic, a tramp", she decided that it was actually this man that she should be making. The experience with the tramp was one of the high points in the process for Regina. The following is what took place.

The room in which we met for the first part of the evening was divided into two sections: firstly, dark and closed; and, secondly, open and light. After a silent meditation, at the point of being as empty of thought and expectation as possible, we let ourselves be guided to either side of the room, and to be in that "dark and closed" and "open and light" space through movement, letting arise what needed to arise. At any point in this exploration one was free to move to the opposite side of the room, embodying that quality of energy as well. Within the period of time allotted for the exercise, there was no limit to how long one spent on either side, or to how many times one crossed the boundary between one side of the room and the other. One was also free to straddle both sides, dark and light, simultaneously – all in whatever form of movement or embodiment, including sound, that evinced itself. Here in this room of lightness and darkness, the alcoholic tramp was born.

Regina says of her experience, *"Ich war er. Er war ich."* "I was he. He was I." And through him she learned much. He was ill, an alcoholic with heart trouble. But in spite of being sick, he was full of life and had no fear. He knew that he was addicted and that he was going to die, but he was not afraid of death. He was able to let go of his fears and his sadness in spite of his life-threatening situation. The *Landstreicher's* presence helped Regina to let go of some of her own fears, as well as some of the strict demands that she had placed on herself. Through this humble yet profound encounter she was shown that one can be ill, and yet be happy and fulfilled at the same time. He showed her that one is allowed to be happy, even when one is not perfect. *"Man darf."* "One is allowed." It seemed reasonable that such an important figure would be the logical choice for coming into manifestation as her inner figure.

During our Christmas break, I asked everyone to choose an image with which to work for the two-week period that we were not meeting. In whatever way felt appropriate and important for each person, they were to focus on their chosen image as often as they found it possible, to let it grow within them. Regina chose the image of a waterfall, which she sat by for long periods of time in the countryside in silence. She both painted and wrote about her experiences. She had never before worked so intensively with only one word, or image. In the intensive contemplation of falling water, of water falling, releasing itself with abandon into a joy-filled expression of life, she came to experience what is so difficult, if not impossible, to put into words: the connection to her *Göttlichkeit*, to her Godliness, to Godliness itself. The words that did come to her were these:

"And God saw all that He had made; and He saw that it was good."

Regina's ability to sense and more fully acknowledge an abiding Presence was taking root and growing in many of the experiences to which she was led in her process with the figure. The joy-filled tramp, living in fearless and loving abandon to life, and to death; the water revealing its splendor and beauty by the surrender of its falling. These were teachers in Regina's growing capacity to offer herself in trust to the Absolute Ground of Being. Falling and failing were becoming less fearsome.

The *Landstreicher* was still strong in Regina's mind as the candidate for her inner figure; then, three months into the process, an unexpected and moving image came to Regina during a subsequent meditation. She saw the apparition of a nun floating above a burning bush. Regina notes that the nun was just as fiery and alive in temperament as the burning of the bush. Shortly after beginning to reflect on this image, Regina realized, *"Jetzt!"* "Now! This is the figure I must make." Without having the vaguest idea of why she should be making a nun, rather than her dearly beloved alcoholic tramp, she set out – like trusting Vasalisa with doll in pocket, guiding her through the darkness of the forest – to make the nun. She, like the surrendering fall of water, put pure trust in the image that came from the unconscious, as well as in the inner voice that said, "Now! This is the figure I must make." Regina with the Nun is illustrated in Figure 8.1.

Figure 8.1 Regina with Nun (Photographed by Thomas Bichsel)

And so she proceeded to make the nun. *She also began to make a baby for the nun.* This second decision was an act of radical trust. She simply knew, for no rational reason whatsoever, that the nun must have a baby in her arms.

At this point, I would like to tell you what Regina shared with me regarding her parents and her childhood.

In the earliest years of her life, during the war, Regina lived with her mother and her brother. Eventually, she came to meet an uncle whom they visited on a farm in a far-off village. Regina was three. She spent many lovely hours with her uncle, whom she very much loved; and it was clear to Regina that he loved her as well, with the greatest affection and tenderness. One day her uncle came to live with them. It was only then that she was told: he was her father. Because he was, as a well-known politician, in danger of being captured and imprisoned by the allies occupying Germany, his identity and whereabouts had to be kept secret. At such a young age, Regina could not be entrusted with the knowledge that this was her father. She could have inadvertently revealed him. After coming home, however, Regina's relationship with her uncle-turned-father changed dramatically. He no longer seemed to have any time for her; the tenderness which she experienced with her "uncle" had disappeared completely. She could remember not one affectionate caress from him as her father. She realizes now that in returning home he came into the reality of a broken life and all its overwhelming difficulties. Once a very rich man, he was now poor. His time was spent in preoccupation with his shattered life and with his own individual interests, which included many hours of reading and studying a vast diversity of subjects including philosophy, ancient history, and the arcane.

For many years Regina tried, in vain, to regain her father's love and affection. But he simply had no time for his family. Finally, when Regina was 18 years old, her father was able to come out of his self-imposed cloistering and expressed a desire to share his life and love with his children, with Regina. But she was no longer interested in being close to him. She was well-behaved, polite, but unable to forgive him for what he had done. It was only at his death that forgiveness and intimacy were in some way restored. Regina was in Switzerland when he called for her to come to Germany. He wanted to see her. He waited for her to come before he finally died. His death was a redemption of their estranged relationship. "He showed me a beautiful death. Peaceful, quiet. I am grateful to him for that. He didn't show me how to live, but he showed me how to die."

Years later, Regina re-read the many journals that her father had written when he was in hiding at the farmer's house. She had read them once before, but it was only upon reading them a second time, much later, that she understood what he was writing. *Er war sehr gottgläubig.* "He believed very much in God." "And knew many things about nature, the cosmos, things he couldn't show or explain to me." Regina's sense of loss was even more poignant at this new-found realization; it touched an even deeper nerve. To have missed sharing those ideas with him, to have missed learning those precious things from him in childhood, has been a great source of suffering for Regina.

Regina's relationship with her mother was also in some ways distanced. Being the lively and playful child did not always endear Regina to her mother who had a more reserved manner. *"Ich schwamm gegen den Strom."* "I swam against the stream." There was always an undercurrent of conflict. There was never a sense of identity with her mother, a sense of being bonded with her. Although Regina feels her mother to be a good person, being overlooked – in favor of her brother or others – has been a consistent experience for Regina in relationship to her mother, and is only one of the many ways in which she realizes that maternal presence has been less than enough. The sense of abandonment is pervasive. Regina's mother had no milk for her when she was born. Shortly after they arrived home from the hospital, a wetnurse had to be employed. That was the second early abandonment Regina experienced. The first brings us directly back to her inner figure, the nun.

The last phase of making the doll requires that one either make or buy clothing for the figure. Since Regina cannot sew she decided to ask her mother for help. She went to Germany and said she needed a nun's habit for her doll.

> "A nun? You're making a nun?"
>   "Yes, a nun."
> "Why?"
>   "I don't know why."
> "A nun … a nun …. Why a nun? Oh! Of course you're making a nun! Of course!"

And then, for the first time, the story unfolded.

When Regina was born, her mother had chosen a private clinic in which to give birth. It was a private clinic run by nuns. Her mother had been partially anaesthetized for the delivery, so as to experience less pain and discomfort. Immediately after Regina was born, there was a bombing raid. Because her mother was exhausted from the birth and (due to the anaesthesia) unable to attend to her new child, one of the nuns took Regina into her arms and went down into the cellar with her, where she stayed for the first critical hours of her life. It was, as a newborn infant, *in the arms of the nun,* that Regina was sheltered from harm, and where she felt the first impulses of love and concern. While she had been inadvertently abandoned by her mother, she had felt the harbouring arms of the nun as her salvation in the maelstrom and trauma of sudden separation and bombing. The deeper meaning of Regina's spontaneous vision of a nun hovering over a burning bush finally revealed itself; and her irrational, though emphatic, impulse to make a baby for the nun's arms was no longer a naggingly quizzical notion. Regina's inner figure, appearing as it did, revealed, as well as embodied, a profound mystery in her life.

The unconscious had stored this experience, to be uncovered in this very unexpected and numinous way. But for what reason? What was Regina to understand from this awe-inspiring and synchronistic event? Regina remembers that whenever she was sad or troubled she would go to the *Kloster*, to the monastery, where the nuns lived. *"Kloster heißt Friede, Liebe."* "The monastery means peace, love." These first moments in her life, surrounded by the peace and protection she experienced in the arms of the nun, embodied the love and sense of redemption she had continually sought throughout her early life. Retrieving the experience of the nun with Regina-as-baby in her arms was the retrieving of the experience of love and salvation. Through the numen of this synchronistic event, love was made more conscious in Regina's life. "I could as well have made a Christ figure. The nun is an image of Christ for me." Through the numinosity and depth of her experience, Regina is much more certain of her belief in God, *Gottesglaube*, those things about which her father wrote so passionately. "I am more conscious now that God lives in me. I am aware of that power in me. And with this assurance, a growing sense of wisdom, understanding and tolerance, the ability to just let things be as they are, including myself." Just like her beloved *Landstreicher* was able to do.

Cedrus … and Peter

> Like stars, mists and candleflames,
> Mirages, dew-drops and water bubbles
> Like dreams, lightning and clouds.
> In that way will I view all composite phenomena.

> Tibetan Wishing Prayer

The making of my last figure had progressed without much event until the modelling of the face. There was something definitely different that needed to happen, I felt, in this figure. It happened one evening, while I was working on the eyes. I took one of the modelling tools and pushed the clay so that the eyes slanted upwards. At first, in their rough unrefined form, the eyes looked other-worldly. After working on them for an hour, I realized they were Asian eyes. I then soon realized I was making a monk; and even more to the point, I was making a spiritual teacher. In the tradition of Asian monks, I decided to make the face to include a bald head, as well as ears, all of porcelain, all in one piece. This was the first time this had occurred in the figure-making as I knew it. The first stages of Tara's face are illustrated in Figure 8.2.

All our porcelain pieces – hands, feet and faces – were finally finished and were brought to the artist who would fire them in his large kiln. There is always the possibility that something will go wrong in the firing: a piece can crack, or worse, explode, thereby endangering other pieces. One never knows, so one prays. On this occasion the artist had fired the clay at the highest temperature possible. This yields a beautiful, translucent, stone-like quality that only porcelain can have when fired at such high temperatures. After about three weeks of waiting, the pieces were returned, all intact. We could breath again. As I looked at my figure's head,

Figure 8.2 First Stages of Tara's face and head (Photographed by Thomas Bichsel)

however, I realized it had become "distorted". The high temperature was too much for the thin and delicate cranium to withstand. It had collapsed slightly, becoming narrower, and along with it, the face. My monk, I saw, had turned into a woman. At first I was petulant, embarrassingly so. I completely forgot myself as I stood moaning and whining about my piece in front of the other course participants. No one could help noticing my reaction, least of all myself. I stopped short. What was I doing? Apart from the disaster of a completely destroyed piece, I had always told people that these things happen as part of the figure. And now I was ignoring my own counsel, letting my ego desires run nakedly rampant. After I was able to stop long enough to reflect on what had happened, I realized that what I had called "distorted" was not a distortion at all, but rather a transformation. And within that transformation, a message. But what was the figure trying to tell me? Where was my thinking "distorted", rather than the piece? That was what I had to discover.

Within a very short time, I realized that this figure was, indeed, a spiritual teacher. I had never had that kind of reaction to the so-called aberrations that might have presented themselves in my figures. She was teaching me in a new way to more fully accept what is. What is more, and even more specific to her lesson, I realized the following: I had always looked to men as spiritual teachers. I had never looked to a woman for that role. But the figure was, without question, both before *and after* the transformation of gender, a spiritual teacher. That the teacher had changed from male to female made me stop, realize, and *admit* how ready I have been to regard the spiritual teachings of and by a woman as somehow inferior, or at least not quite as important, or accomplished, as that which might be transmitted by a man. Intellectually, publicly, and without being conscious of the contradiction within me, I would have vehemently denied this. But secretly, deep down in my soul, I knew I had to admit that is what I felt. It took this figure to put that destructive prejudice unavoidably in my face (if you will excuse the pun). For several days thereafter, I felt both saddened and disturbed by what had been revealed by this event. The sadness soon abated, however, as I became more and more aware of the gift of my figure's teachings, and all that could (and would) follow as a result.

Without knowing exactly who *Tara* was at the time, other than the primary female deity of compassion in the Tibetan Buddhist tradition, I referred to my doll as a Tara figure. Later, I discovered that Tara is the principle female Bodhisattva in Tibetan Buddhism: she is the female aspect of the Buddha, i.e., the Buddha, or the Fully Enlightened, *in female form*.

About six months after completing this figure, which I will refer to as *Tara*, I began to talk with my friend, Rachael Wooten, about her. I do not recall now exactly how it was that we began the conversations, but I am certain it was because of Rachael's active interest in Tibetan Buddhism that the dialogue started. After hearing me refer to *Tara* and describing her, and after hearing a landmark dream I had had in 1982 about the 16th Karmapa (who holds for one sect in Tibetan Buddhism a similar position as the Dalai Lama holds for all the sects), Rachael told me that I should see her teacher, Lama Lodro, Abbot of the Tibetan Monastery in Switzerland, and tell him my dream. I was extremely hesitant. It seemed too personal an issue

Figure 8.3 Original gilded-bronze statue of Avalokiteshvara (two views, photographed by Michael Drobný)

to bother him with, although, since meeting the Karmapa in Santa Fe, New Mexico, in 1979, I had wanted to become actively involved in Tibetan Buddhism for years. The door, however, never seemed to open fully enough for me to enter, for whatever reason. Rachael not only continued to encourage me to see the Abbot of the monastery, but also asked Lama Lodro directly if it would be appropriate to see him and recount my dream. He responded in the affirmative. Finally, after all these years – after the making of *Tara* – the door opened.

Before going on to say what happened when I finally went to see Lama Lodro, I would like to explain that Rachael was, and is, firmly convinced of women's equal value in relationship to men, both in the transmission of spiritual teachings and otherwise. It has been primarily through my friendship with Rachael that my relationship to the Feminine, in this regard, has shifted. *Tara* was my link to Rachael; Rachael was my link to Lama Lodro; and Lama Lodro was my direct link to the teachings. Not surprisingly (for this story), the first major teaching from Lama Lodro was to receive from him *The Initiation of The Twenty-One Taras* (*Tara* has twenty-one different aspects or emanations) and to receive, through it, the devotional practices that are recited to the feminine aspect of the Buddha. I was now in the position to express and experience spiritual devotion to the Divine Feminine through a grounded, rooted tradition to which I felt inexplicably but unequivocally connected. What is very important to the synchronistic nature of the events is that it was Rachael and her discussions with Lama Lodro that had inspired the giving of *The Initiation of The Twenty-One Taras*, which was consequently made available to the entire Tibetan Buddhist community in the area of Zürich. I had been led very carefully to the lap of the Mother, the Spiritual Mother, who provides nourishment not primarily for the body, but for the development of one's spiritual life.

Very pertinent to the story, and certainly not just a coincidental occurrence, is the fact that it was precisely at this time that the relationship with my own personal mother began to take new form. We have always been close, the relationship always intense. We have grown, suffered, and rejoiced with one another. And yet, some of the deepest wounds were still in the process of healing. In the period of time during which I became actively involved with Tibetan Buddhism and received *The Initiation of the Twenty-One Taras*, long-standing and somewhat intractable wounds were addressed more deeply than at any other time, and began to heal. (Of course, it must also be said that nearly seven years of Jungian analysis with Dr. Helmut Barz is the solid and irreplaceable psychic backbone of this development.) Although we are still mother and daughter, and always will be, we are freer than ever before to stand independent of one another, each respecting the life and autonomy of the other, each having more compassion for the other. The Spiritual Mother presides between us.

Returning now to my initial meeting with Lama Lodro, I finally took up my courage and made an appointment to see him. In this first meeting, I recounted my dream of the 16th Karmapa. I told Lama Lodro that the Karmapa had appeared in a dream during an extreme physical crisis in which I was very close to death; the Karmapa seemed to have aroused the energies of healing through his presence in the dream, enough so that I was able to recover and call for the much needed care and medical assistance I had originally resisted. After hearing the dream to its completion, Lama Lodro's response was that there had clearly been previous connections with Tibetan Lamas and Buddhist teachings in former lives; he graciously invited me to participate, once again, in *this* one. I began then to tell him about the figure I had made of *Tara*. Before I could explain in any detail, he interrupted and asked me quite spontaneously; "Figures? You make figures? I'm in need of a figure. Can you make one for me?" I was dumbfounded. Not only was I aware that the figures I made were very different from the figures he had in mind, which are actually statues, but I was totally taken off guard by his immediate, trusting and direct request. After responding with a flurry of excuses about how I did not make statues, had never made *any* statue, and did not know if I could ever make what he wanted (and simultaneously thinking to myself feverishly the whole while that I did not have any *time* to do this) … I said yes. I had suddenly realized I was being given a teaching, the nature of which I did not know, but could not refuse. The next time I saw him, he put a centuries-old, gilded-bronze figure in front of me and told me I could take it home to use as a model. Once again, I was speechless. I took it home, photographed it, then returned it, using the photos as the model. I started, then, on my long sojourn into the unknown.

It took approximately 220 hours to model the figure of porcelain clay, over a period of four to five months. It stands 22 centimeters tall. The statue includes a base in the form of a lotus blossom, a lion which sits on the base, and *Avalokiteshvara*, the Buddha of Compassion, who sits atop the lion. I documented the making of the figure, including my experiences and dreams, while constructing it. What seems appropriate to recount is the fact that quite often, just before going to sleep and upon arising, I would receive information about how to put the figure together. I did not know how to do it; I had never worked in this way before. But I was guided, shown step by step, as to how I should accomplish my task. In a somewhat miraculous way, it seemed, the figure came to completion after many long weeks of work that, although intense, proceeded without any insurmountable problem. Once again, dumbfounded. The original and reproduction statues of the Buddha of Compassion are illustrated in Figure 8.3 and Figure 8.4.

There were many things I learned while making this statue, the nature and mystery of which feel inexpressible, or would at least seem reductive in the telling. What I can say is that the compassion which *Avalokiteshvara* embodies began to touch my life in the deepest ways. A widening sense of compassion, not only for others but also for my own inconsistencies, flaws and failures, began to flow more freely. It seemed that the very heart of *Vajrayana* Buddhism was finding its invincible way to mine through the making of this figure.

The statue complete, I brought it to Lama Lodro. I had told him previously that since I had had no experience with glazing a piece like this, I would deliver it in its pure, unglazed, or white, state. He said fine, he would paint it. When I delivered the statue, however, he said he needed to find someone who would do the painting. I was a bit confused, but that was not unusual. I recovered, and immediately suggested that Peter, my husband, might offer to do it for him. I called Peter on the spot. After five seconds of deliberation, he said yes. I could tell he knew it was a teaching for him as well. With Lama Lodro enthusiastically nodding and smiling me a farewell, I left his chamber and brought the statue back home for Peter to paint.

Originally, Peter thought it would be a relatively quick and simple process to paint the statue. But it was to be otherwise. After several long weeks of being unable to approach the painting, he finally settled into the process. In the end, he spent almost as much time painting the statue as I had taken to model it. And the teachings that came along with the painting were some of the most intense, and searing, either of us has ever experienced. It had not been destined to be a quick and simple, or painless, process. Peter and I have been married for 13 years. We met each other as a result of our mutual interest in image-making. This has been one of our strongest bonds throughout our relationship. No matter what else has happened between us, we have always been able to put aside our differences in our work as artists. What happened as a result of working on the statue together seems to have been no exception, but this time our ability to put our differences aside occurred in an extraordinary and totally unexpected way.

In our best moments, which are many, Peter and I are the most committed of friends, respectful of each other's individuality and humanity. In our most difficult moments with each other (or as a result thereof), we have both understood how easy it is to lose almost all touch with human decency, and to feel the most abject sense of hatred possible for another human being. We have had that very difficult and tortuous experience with each other three times in our relationship. The first time it happened, we found our way through it, in spite of the near catastrophic state of devastation we felt as a result. The experience left us reeling; our survival of it, however, created an almost irrevocable bond of trust. The last two instances came while Peter was painting the statue. It was during these two traumatic events that we were given the invaluable opportunity to find our way – but only with the greatest of psychic and spiritual effort – into an unparalleled (for us) experience of compassion, not only for each other, but for ourselves, individually, as well. Conscious, authentic self-forgiveness and self-love can sometimes be the most difficult inner experiences to attain. It was working with the statue, and with the teachings it represents in image form, that brought us to this experience.

I already mentioned this above, but I believe it bears repeating here: the deity of the statue, *Avalokiteshvara*, is the Buddha of Compassion. It is this aspect of the Buddha that the Dalai Lama incarnates. Furthermore, it is this aspect of the Buddha that the Karmapa, the Lama of whom I dreamt, and with whom I took my initial Buddhist vows, also incarnates. Through Lama Lodro and his request for the statue, the Karmapa's and the Buddhist teachings found their way to me again – indeed, to both Peter and myself – providing the necessary experiences for generating the healing powers of compassion, the heart of *Vajrayana*, or Tibetan Buddhism.

With the entrance of *Tara* into my personal process of *The Inner Figure*, I was led to these experiences I describe. *Tara* is associated with the element of ether. It is said that when one is in distress and when one fervently calls her for help, *Tara* will come immediately, the element

Figure 8.4 Reproduction of gilded-bronze statue made by Cedrus and Peter (two views, photographed by Peter Andréas Ziermann)

of ether being omnipresent and moving faster than the wind. Perhaps the making of *Tara* was an unconscious call made conscious, leading to a shocking though healing experience of the numinous.

It has been said that enlightenment is the state of being unhindered in one's actions. Lama Lodro seemed to have been unhindered in the act of requesting the making and painting of this statue. In this unhindered state, he gave both Peter and me the possibility of receiving teachings that we would never otherwise have experienced.

Lama Lodro has been instrumental in furthering the figure-making process. There is now a very important, additional aspect to *The Inner Figure*, both in ideology and in practice, and I am certain that what has been learned through the gift of this experience will continue to be incorporated into *The Inner Figure* process.

*
* *

There is in the soul of humankind a power of imagination which can produce concrete changes in matter. For the alchemist it was the matter contained within the retort; for the shaman, the alterations occur in nature where stones speak. Changes of this nature occur in *The Inner Figure* process as well, when the image-maker transforms the matter of his or her own being through the making and manifestation of the soul's image.

References

Estés, Clarissa Pinkola (1992). *Women Who Run With the Wolves.* New York: Ballantine Books.

Jung, C.G. (1989). *The Collected Works.* Ed. Sir Herbert Read, Michael Fordham, and Gerhard Adler. Routledge: London; Second Edition, reprinted in 1989; Volumes 6, 8, 12.

Jung, C.G. (1973). *Letters: Vol. 1, Vol. 2.* Ed. Gerhard Adler, Aniela Jaffé; trans. R.F.C. Hull. Routledge and Kegan Paul: London.

Keene, Donald (1965). *Bunraku: The Art of Japanese Puppet Theatre.* Kodansha International Ltd.: New York.

von Franz, Marie-Louise (1973/1995). *Creation Myths.* Shambhala: Boston and London.

von Franz, Marie-Louise (1980). *Divination and Synchronicity: The Psychology of Meaningful Chance.* Inner City Books: Toronto, Canada.

von Franz, Marie-Louise (1992). *Psyche and Matter.* Shambhala: Boston and London.

9

The Alchemy of Art in Analysis

by Joy Schaverien

It is sometimes stated as a negative of the therapeutic encounter that pictures in analysis seduce the analyst. In this chapter I intend to explore this. It is my premise that pictures can and sometimes do seduce both analyst and analysand and that far from this being a negative indication, it is one of the essential elements when pictures are made in the context of an analytic relationship. I propose that, unless the picture does have the power to seduce the analyst, it is unlikely to be an effective element in the treatment. Such seduction is rarely overt; it may be subtle or unconscious, and it is only one of the aesthetic effects of pictures made within the analytic frame. I will show how Jung's alchemical metaphor for the transference relates when pictures are involved in analysis. My intention is to demonstrate, through clinical example, how the temporary seduction of the analyst, through the picture, may be a beneficial phase in an analysis. I propose that, consciously handled, it may facilitate a process of transformation.

I will draw on Jung's *Psychology of the Transference* (Jung, 1946) to help elucidate my understanding of the transference within the pictures. In Jungian circles it is well understood that the alchemical metaphor which Jung applied in that text is a useful means of understanding the subtle interplay of the transference and countertransference relationship in psychotherapy. However, I do not think that the link with pictures in analysis has been made in the way I propose. The connection is that, like the artist, the alchemists were working with actual chemical substances which were transformed by the processes to which they were subjected. This practice had a spiritual as well as practical aim and, as with art in analysis, the transformations of the base metals had their counterpart in the inner world of the adept. Thus I am proposing Jung's link with alchemy may help our understanding of the ways in which art might influence the transference. The pretty chocolate-box image, to which some analysands initially aspire, does not have the power to seduce the viewer. Nor does it transform the inner world in the sense which I have in mind. Conversely the raw, untamed and sometimes unnameable image, which at first glance may not look at all pretty, may well have the power to do so. This is an aesthetic consideration, which we might recognise if we recall that which is pleasing in art viewed in a "public" setting such as an art gallery. The initial appeal of a work of art, private or public, is an attraction which invites the viewer to make a closer inspection. Subsequently a successful work provokes a response. To have such an effect a picture will have substance and it will convey a tension; it will embody the essence of a dynamic opposition. It is an "embodied image".

The distinction I have made elsewhere (Schaverien 1987, 1991) between the embodied and the diagrammatic image is relevant. This distinction is a result of considering the aesthetic qualities of different types of pictures created within the analytic context (Schaverien 1995, 1998). The *diagrammatic* image is usually made consciously to convey an idea or a feeling state (Schaverien 1987, p. 77, 1991, p. 86). Such a picture is very often like a sign and, like the chocolate box image mentioned above, it refers to something outside of itself. It may play a significant part in analysis by bringing material to light but it needs explanation in words in order to convey its full meaning. The diagrammatic image may be an aid to speaking about a situation but – and this is my point – in the process of its creation nothing changes.

The *embodied image* is different; it is an image which could have no other form; it reveals a state which cannot be spoken. In the process of its creation something changes at a profound level; perhaps the artist sets out with the intention of doing one thing and finds out that something else has emerged in the process. This I have argued is a form of transference, the "scapegoat transference" where feeling becomes live within the therapeutic relationship, but is contained within the picture. Such an embodied picture may well disturb the artist, as viewer of her or his own work. It may also profoundly affect the analyst and so evoke a countertransference response. The viewer may identify with the image or reject it, but whatever the response, the point is that an aesthetically engaging piece of work will not leave the viewer unmoved.

The aesthetic experience can only be appreciated with a suspension of desire, as well as of judgement, according to Kant (1790). This very assertion implies that there is some tendency to desire something from the experience of viewing a picture. It is similar in analysis. Freud recognised the desire of the analysand when he came to understand "Transference Love" (Freud 1912, 1915), and the topic of desire has been approached by many analysts since. Most agree with Freud that it is the abstinence from acting on the desire which transforms the inner world of the client. Bion, in his much quoted phrase (Bion 1970, p. 41), states that an absence of memory and desire is essential in the psychoanalyst if he/she is to be available for the analysand in the present. It seems that the aesthetics of art and of psychoanalysis require a similar attitude.

At first this seems paradoxical. It is when the desire of the client enters the therapeutic encounter that analysis comes alive and so change is possible; it is then that the analyst's desire becomes engaged and inevitably both people are affected and changed. And yet it is the absence of desire and of memory which is required. Perhaps this is not really so very paradoxical, for to be able to work in the present the analyst must first relinquish her need for the analysand. This might be a need for the analysand to get better, or for the analysand as an "ideal" partner; or for any combination of conscious or unconscious needs which may be evoked. It is clear that the analyst enters this work with a need to heal some part of her or himself; the wounded healer is an acknowledged aspect of the process (Sedgwick, 1994). The purpose of the training analysis is to bring these aspects of the analyst's inner world to consciousness. This makes it less likely that the analyst will burden the analysand with her or his unconscious needs and reparative love. My intention is to attempt to develop this awareness in relation to art in analysis.

I propose that when pictures are presented or made in analysis, the transference to the picture, the "scapegoat transference", adds an element within the therapeutic relationship. There are then two linked strands to the transference. The first is the transference to the person of the analyst and the second the transference *embodied* in the picture. These threads of the transference both have their complement in separate but linked strands of the countertransference. For example the analyst may feel "drawn in" to the picture. It may be that the analyst and analysand are literally "drawn in" the picture in representational or symbolic ways, but it may be subtler and less conscious than this. I will show a series of "embodied images" which played a central part within the therapeutic relationship. The link with the transference is graphically revealed in this case because the imagery resonates with the woodcuts from *The Psychology of the Transference* (Jung, 1946).

The Psychology of the Transference

In *The Psychology of the Transference* Jung shows a series of woodcuts which he discovered in an ancient alchemical text, *The Rosarium Philosophorum* (Jung, 1946). Jung equates this text with stages in the transference and countertransference in depth psychology. In the woodcuts the alchemical (or analytic) journey is pictured through the transformations in the (psychological) relationship of two people. The couple are the alchemist and his assistant. In psychotherapy Jung intended them to be seen as both the analysand and analyst in the transference, and aspects of the individual psyche (Samuels 1985, p. 181). Although it may at first seem esoteric, unworldly and perhaps irrelevant to our present-day concerns, it is an image which Jungians understand as a metaphor for the unconscious meeting in the analytic encounter (Edinger, 1985; Jacoby, 1984; Schwartz-Salant, 1989; Samuels, 1989).

The opus of the alchemist was a quest, the aim of which was the transformation of base metals into gold. The process involved the combining of diverse elements in a vessel. This vessel was known by several different names, among which was the uterus, for it was within the dark waters of this vessel that the philosopher's stone, the lapis, was distilled. The chemical elements were drawn together by an affinity – a chemical combination. This affinity first attracts and then binds the two substances, transforming both in the process – the two becoming one. This alchemical mix, or "marriage", which is the centre of the opus, is known as the *coniunctio*. In the woodcuts this is symbolised as a sexual union.

Jung regarded this process as a metaphor for the intense feelings sometimes evoked within the therapeutic relationship. He suggests that the unconscious interaction in the transference / countertransference dynamic is similar to the attraction of opposites of the chemical interaction in alchemy. Thus the analyst and analysand may be drawn into an intimate form of relatedness irrespective of their conscious wishes. The *coniunctio* here is the combination of unconscious elements from the psyche of the analysand, which unite with unconscious elements from the psyche of the analyst.

The Outer Vessel – the Relationship

The analytic relationship is the vessel in which this *coniunctio* takes place and, like the alchemical vessel, this too is sealed. The boundaries and limits of the setting, the confidentiality and the undivided attention of the analyst, contribute to this. Within the analytic vessel there may be an affinity which draws the two people together. In order to become susceptible to this the analyst lowers her or his consciousness, permitting the influence of the analysand to permeate her or his being. There is an intensity when the unconscious of the analysand meets the unconscious of the analyst and, at times, an incestuous atmosphere may draw the analyst, in spite of himself, into a repetition of the family dynamics of the analysand. In this way, through the countertransference, the neurosis of the analysand temporarily infects the analyst. The unconscious elements in the psyche of the analysand are then mediated through the analyst and brought out into the light of consciousness.

The Alchemy of Pigments

As already suggested, when pictures are brought to analysis, or made within the analytic setting, Jung's metaphor may be extended. The artwork may become an additional vessel within which the unconscious elements meet and mix. There are two stages; the first is the transference, which the analysand makes to the picture, in the process of its creation. Like the alchemist, the artist is working with materials which are mixed, combined, and eventually transformed from the original disparate substances into a unified whole. The base elements of this "alchemy" are the artist's materials: the paint, canvas, charcoal and paper and, in sculpture, the clay and water or the metals used for casting. Furthermore, if we consider the colours that are used in painting we realise that they too are made from metals. A glance at the common names given to artist's paints reveals this. For example: titanium white, chrome yellow, cobalt blue, cadmium red or yellow indicate the metals on which they are based. The ochres, such as yellow and red ochre, are natural earths and burnt umber and sienna are colours obtained by roasting the materials. The point is that we might understand these as the substances of the artist's alchemy. These are mixed, combined and synthesised.

The artwork need not be beautiful or even acceptable. The alchemist's journey led to contact with decay, putrefaction and death, before the ultimate goal could be attained. Similarly, the pictures may, at times, be messy, unattractive and even repulsive but this is merely part of the process. A transforming factor is the quality of the engagement of the artist with the painting. It is the *embodied image*, rather than the *diagrammatic*, which facilitates this depth of engagement. This is arrived at spontaneously and cannot be demanded; it is impossible to ask someone to make an embodied image. It is the depth of engagement of the artist with the materials that "draws" the artist into her or his own picture and her/his desire becomes engaged. This desire is for the making of psyche or soul (Hillman, 1972) and it is this for which both painting and analyst supply the necessary external factor.

Like alchemy, it is the human element in art that combines and so transforms the inert substances into volatile and mobile ones. In turn, and again like alchemy, the picture transforms the psyche of the artist, through its very existence. The picture making process mediates. The *coniunctio* between the artist and the materials thus constitutes the first transference in analysis when art is involved. However, in order for this process to be contained, mediated and finally integrated within the personality of the analysand, interpretation of the transference to the analyst is essential at some point. This process is facilitated by the containing aspects of the pictures, as a form of inner vessel, within the analytic frame.

The Art Object as Inner Vessel

As in any other form of analysis, the analyst and the setting form a containing vessel which permits what is within to be as chaotic as necessary. However, I am proposing that when art is a factor in analysis it forms an additional containing vessel, but within the outer frame provided by the analyst and the setting.

In painting, the paper or canvas provides the vessel in which certain marks and colour combinations may be made. In sculpture it may be the clay, wood or stone which is the vessel from which the forms emerge. The affinity, the attraction that brings these elements together, is the attraction of the artist for a particular combination of marks, forms or colours. It is the artist who chooses to place cadmium red beside ultramarine, for example, and, in this juxtaposition, both colours are transformed; the appearance of each is altered by the proximity of the other. It is through the lengthy process of distilling and altering such relationships that the work is eventually created. Like alchemy this process has a depth-psychological parallel. This is the first part of the process.

The second stage is when the completed picture is viewed. The process now attends to the object nature of art as well as the imagery which it reveals and so the picture becomes the vessel for the transforming mix – but in a different way. No longer is the volatile element the combination of material substances. The picture now becomes a vessel for the mixing of the gaze of analysand and analyst. Further this leads to the mixing of conscious and unconscious elements from the psyche of the artist with those of the analyst. This is a result of the imagery that the picture reveals. The forms, figurations and relationships within the picture are made by the analysand but they may also reflect and incorporate unconscious elements of the therapeutic relationship. For example they may have been made with an awareness of the analyst as viewer. The analyst may consciously or possibly unconsciously recognise these elements. Especially if they are alive in the transference they may have the effect of drawing her/him into the picture. If the material in the picture is of an archetypal nature this may be intensified. A pattern is discernible in such material, which combines aspects of the personal and the collective unconscious. Analysand and analyst may both be attracted to such a picture because there is an unconscious recognition that it expresses the nature of their mutual relatedness. This is the alchemical "mix" which takes place within the vessel of the picture. This might be considered to be a form of seduction through the picture. However, it is also significant as an aesthetic form of countertransference, temporarily centred in the picture.

The Woodcuts

The woodcuts on which *The Psychology of the Transference* is based correspond in many ways with the pictures made by the client, which I will show. The first illustration in the series, the Mercurial Fountain, is the vessel containing the *prima materia* or the divine water, in which the elements are understood to combine. In the second the opposing elements are shown as the sun and the moon, on which stand the king and queen. They are also a brother-sister pair and, although they are clothed, Jung writes that an incestuous connection is revealed in the contact of their left hands. In the next illustration they are naked. Then, as the process deepens, they are shown immersed in the bath which is the mercurial fountain. The transformation is continued in several pictures where they are depicted in copulation. The soul, in the form of a child, departs leaving a state of stasis, the *mortifactio*, a near-death state. The child returns symbolising rebirth, and eventually the disparate parts of the self are united. They come together anew as is shown by the androgynous figure, which is the alchemical marriage.

132

The woodcuts are well known and so they are not all reproduced here. I refer the interested reader to the original work by Jung (1946) or to my own fuller discussion of them (Schaverien, 1991). For this chapter I have selected the three which relate directly to the pictures I have chosen to show. Jung states that the stages, which he describes, seem to correspond to inner psychological reasons in the individual case (Jung, 1946), and he makes the point that they do not necessarily appear in the same sequence as the woodcuts. This is the case with the pictures below. In them the stages described by Jung can be recognised but they are like layers, which overlap and at times interweave with each other. The pictures reveal both the inner journey and the pattern of the relationship in the transference.

These eight pictures are selected from over 200 made by this client, thirty-two of which were shown in *The Revealing Image* (Schaverien, 1991). These pictures illuminate the topic of this paper and so, although they were made many years ago in my art therapy practice, I consider that the unconscious processes which they reveal are similar to those which emerge in my current analytic practice. One reason that these pictures are shown here is because I have analysed them in detail elsewhere. At the time they were made, as with many pictures in analysis, neither the artist / analysand nor the analyst knew what they meant. However, both knew that they were significant. It is only years later, having analysed the series of pictures within the context of the others, that I have some sense of their meaning. It is always thus with pictures; they need to be regarded as a whole. They need time to speak their own particular story in the context of the therapeutic relationship. Too quick attribution of meaning to the individual parts treats them merely as signs. Seen within the context of the whole picture, within the context of the therapeutic relationship, the pictures themselves may be regarded as what Langer (1967) calls the "art symbol". They are then profoundly symbolic, revealing the depths of their psychological impact.

The client whom I call Harry was twenty-four years old when he was admitted to the therapeutic community where I was the art therapist. I will not describe the case in any detail, but it is of note that he was unhappy because he was not fulfilling his potential. He was an intelligent young man but he had difficulty in forming relationships and he was employed in a job which was below his capacities. As the work progressed it emerged that, in part, his problems seemed to derive from his very early experiences when his next sibling had been born. I will not discuss this here, but it was revealed in the transference, through his behaviour and demeanour. However, it was the pictures which revealed the depth of his experience in a way that no words could convey.

The Dancers

The two dancers in Figures 9.1 and 9.2 appeared in the first weeks of therapy and then at regular intervals throughout the four years that we worked together. They were interspersed

Figure 9.1 The Dancers I

with many other pictures, but the theme recurred intermittently throughout the process. It is noticeable that the relationships of the dancers in these pictures alter and change position in relation to each other. The art materials used at this stage are safe, conservative and intimate, pencil and charcoal drawings on paper. Further I consider that they echo the pictures of the alchemical text, which may be demonstrated if we regard Figure 9.1 and Figure 9.2 in relation to the woodcuts in Figure 9.3 and Figure 9.4.

We see that in Jung's pictures (numbered 2 and 3 in *Psychology of the Transference*) the king and queen meet and their left hands touch. The dancers seem to resonate in a similar way. These two pictures were made within a few days of the client's admission to the clinic and so, when, in Figure 9.1, we see the couple meet and face each other it is reminiscent of the actual relationship. The analyst and analysand were meeting and familiarising themselves with each other both consciously and also unconsciously. In Figure 9.2, the couple is drawn with more certainty and they begin to dance. They are on what appears to be both a semi-circular stage and also a bed. They are watched by amorphous figures.

Figure 9.2 The Dancers II

It seems that the analytic dance has begun and this seems to suggest a meeting of elements from the unconscious of the client with those of the analyst. Schwartz-Salant (1989) has proposed that, at the same time as the conscious engagement, there is also an unconscious couple who meet and interact. It seems that this is borne out in the pictures. A couple interacts, seeming to reveal, as Jung (1946) indicates, that within a therapeutic relationship all is not as first appears. It is clear that these are all elements from the client's psyche, but I am suggesting that they were also a product of the therapeutic relationship and, even at this early stage, a reflection of the transference.

To return to Jung's alchemical metaphor, the alchemist had a companion on the journey, usually of the opposite gender. For the man this was known as his *soror mystica* who was sometimes a real person, but at others it was an inner figure (Samuels, 1985). Samuels (1989) emphasises the necessity of the two-person relationship in analysis: "The analyst constellates what is 'other' to consciousness; namely, the unconscious." Thus in the transference the analyst may be seen as this figure, the *soror mystica*, and the split-off or idealised elements in the psyche

135

PHILOSOPHORVM.

Nota bene: In arte noftri magifterij nihil eft *Secretum*
celatũ à Philofophis excepto fecreto artis, quod *artis*
non licet cuiquam reuelare, quod fi fieret ille ma
lediceretur , & indignationem domini incur=
reret , & apoplexia moreretur.   Quare om=
nis error in arte exiftit , ex eo, quod debitam

PHILOSOPHORVM.

feipfis fecundum equalitatẽ infpiffentur. Solus
enim calor tẽperatus eft humiditatis infpiffatiuus
et mixtionis perfectiuus, et non fuper excedens.
Nã generatiões et procreationes rerũ naturaliũ
habent folũ fieri per tẽperatifsimũ calorẽ et equa
lẽ, vti eft folus fimus equinus humidus et calidus.

Figure 9.3 King and Queen

Figure 9.4 The Naked Truth

(Woodcuts from the Rosarium)

may be projected on to her (or him). However, when pictures are centrally involved there is an additional means of resolution. The *coniunctio*, the mixing of conscious and unconscious elements from the psyche of the analysand and analyst, may sometimes take place in the picture. The inner figure, *the soror mystica*, may then appear in the picture. I consider that the dancers reveal this unconscious process and so bring it out into the light of consciousness.

There are two ways this might function within the analytic relationship. Firstly, if the "other" appears in the picture there is an opportunity to work with it as an imaginal figure, because the outer manifestation is in the picture. The analyst may be a witness with the image held in the picture "out there" and separate from both people. It may then be recognised by the analysand as an internal figure or a projection, in which case there is the potential for its reintegration even without overt acknowledgement of the transference.

Figure 9.5 The Foetus

Alternatively, the imagery may engage the analyst in an additionally intense manner, especially if it appears to be associated with herself. The picture may be understood to reveal the analysand's desire and so may evoke a reciprocal countertransference desire. It seems that, as well as the inner world of the analysand, the dancers were also the analysand and analyst beginning the analytic dance and so the analyst was woven into an intimate form of relatedness. The reality of the genders of the pair, in this case, lends itself to this view.

Gender and Anima

The significance of gender is that it is one way in which the opposites manifest themselves. In Jung's view the psyche is made up of opposites; i.e., any conscious attitude is compensated by an unconscious one. These opposites become manifest in culture as well as in the psychological development of the individual. In Jung's writings the feminine is equated with Eros and the masculine with Logos (1959, p. 14). There are aspects of both in men and women which, if they are unconscious, will be projected and attached to a figure of the opposite sex. Thus the unconscious in a man may be characterised by the appearance in his "dreams, visions or fantasies" of an idealised female or "anima" figure who carries the archetypal feminine (Jung, 1959, p. 13/14). The anima is the often, but not exclusively, idealised feminine which leads man towards individuation and to a resolution of a projected part of his personality. This accounts, in part at least, for the incestuous dynamic, which may be experienced in the transference. The projection of the anima may lead to idealisation or else hatred, propelled by the desire for and fear of intimacy, which may be particularly intense for a man working with a female analyst (Schaverien, 1995).

This is how I understand the pictures I have shown here. However, contrary to first impressions there is a complex gender mixing in the psychology of the transference, in which nothing is as it first appears. The story is told through a series of pictures of a heterosexual coupling, but to understand it in merely gender-specific terms would be to miss the complex subtlety of Jung's meaning. The couple represents unconscious elements in the transference and so there is a crossing of gender boundaries; the unconscious of the woman may sometimes manifest itself in male guise and the unconscious of the man in female guise. However, the opposite of the conscious attitude is not always expressed as male / female; there are other such complements to the conscious presentation of the personality. Moreover, if the alchemical pictures are viewed as symbolic of different forms of psychological intercourse they can be understood to be applicable regardless of the reality of the gender or the sexual orientation of the analytic couple. Jung understood Eros to be a purposive aspect of the life-force. Therefore Eros in its widest sense is considered to be a central indicator of the life within the analytic encounter. To be open to this we need to relinquish fixed ideas of gender; it may be that a form of gender uncertainty liberates us to apply this understanding to working in the transference.

This distinction is important because here we are dealing with the feminine and masculine elements in the psychological inner world of a man. The woodcuts and the sense Jung makes of them are like a template, a pattern of understanding of unconscious processes. In Harry's pictures the conscious / unconscious interplay does seem to take the form of male and female elements and it seems that this movement in his inner world was engendered by the transference. Therefore, in this case I consider that the gender of the pair was significant and that the heterosexual pairing led to a particular incestuous dynamic in the transference. The anima figure, which resonated with the transference, was drawn in the picture. This as well as the evident aesthetic qualities of the pictures contributed to the countertransference appeal. The next picture I will discuss is a picture of a foetus.

I suggest that, like the combination of elements in the alchemist's vessel, something new was produced from the initial dance. We have seen that this is not always gold. This picture is very small and painted with intense bright colours, thus the materials affect the impact of the work. The imagery in Figure 9.5 (p. 137) could be understood in several complex ways, one of which is that the foetus, which appears here for the first time, is the "something new" that has come about as the result of the meeting of the dancers. This picture seems to reveal an undeveloped

Figure 9.6 Immersion (Woodcut from the Rosarium)

Figure 9.7 Immersion I

Figure 9.8 Immersion II (Harry's Pictures)

Figure 9.9 Couples I

Figure 9.10 Couples II

aspect of the personality. We might see it as an aspect of the "self" of the analysand, as yet unformed, held within a tear-drop and within a pink heart. The brown semi-circular devices at the corners, in the lower half of the picture, seem to lead the eye of the viewer into the centre. These seem to suggest that the viewer could be looking within the maternal body, or alternatively from the position of the maternal body looking at some unformed element which has been too soon ejected. The sun is far away and blocked off from the foetus by bars and other obstacles.

Clearly this is an aesthetically pleasing picture and this adds to the interest it evokes in the viewer. Within the therapeutic relationship the viewers are the artist / analysand and the analyst. The picture was both made and viewed within the context of the therapeutic relationship and so its aesthetic quality contributes to the countertransference. The picture is of an archetypal nature and thus it engendered both a recognition and engagement from the analyst in relation to its creator.

Immersion

Jung points out that the king and queen are also the brother-sister pair and in Figure 9.6 shown on p. 139 (Figure 4 in *The Psychology of the Transference*) we see them naked and immersed in the vessel.

It is striking that Harry seemed to find similar imagery spontaneously to express his state. The materials used here are coloured felt tip pens on paper. If we regard the picture, Immersion I (Figure 9.7, p. 140), we see a single male figure immersed up to his neck in water. Over his head a single star seems to indicate that this is a special person – this might be viewed as a "self" element, like the foetus. A tree to the left of the picture is light on the left side and dark on the right. A black bird swims to the right of the figure. It reveals the artist alone and it seems to be a somewhat narcissistic image revealing his state, at that time, in a way for which no words could substitute. In this sense it is an embodied image and relates to the transference. The countertransference response was complex, as again these are aesthetically engaging works which at the time were fascinating but also incomprehensible. It is often thus when pictures are first made; it is not possible to understand their meaning. Both analyst and analysand can only wait for meaning to emerge gradually over time.

The second picture, Immersion II (Figure 9.8), was made the following day. Here are two figures, a man and a woman apparently immersed in water. Is it the analyst who is drawn here in the deep water with her client? I would suggest that the answer to this is both yes and also no. On the one hand the picture seems to reveal two aspects of the artist / analysand. The faces of the couple are very similar, indicating that they could be a brother-sister pair and so two aspects of the same person – the analysand. However, I suggest that it could also be seen as the analyst and analysand together in the waters of the unconscious, but also aspects of the individual psyche. The tree has moved to the centre and is between them – light on the male, perhaps solar side – and dark on the female side. Then, if we regard the lower half of the picture, we see a child in a cradle, but barred from the couple. In Figure 7 of the *Rosarium* pictures (not shown here) a child is shown in the dormant state called *impregnatio.*

A further two pictures were made by Harry on consecutive days. The first is a pencil drawing, the second a drawing made with coloured felt tip pens. As we saw earlier in the woodcuts the king and queen (Figures 2 and 3 from the *Rosarium*), are betrothed and the incestuous connection is revealed in the contact of their left hands. In Figure 9.9 (p. 141), the pencil drawing, there are two couples. Perhaps this is the unconscious couple as described by Schwartz-Salant (1989). Although it appears to be a reflection, the two sides of the picture are not identical. The couple on the left appear serious and look out of the picture, a sunset behind them. On the other, lighter side of the tree, the figures smile and the male figure has his left hand raised towards the woman. His left foot is buried in a mound in the ground.

In Figure 9.10, the whole scene is brighter. The couple on the left are white and appear even a little ghostly whilst the couple on the light side of the tree are drawn in colour. He sits on the brown earth-mound, which has now grown larger, wearing the blue and purple lunar colours. The female figure wears the solar yellow colours. In traditional Jungian views this might indicate a crossing of the gender divide or that some intercourse has taken place. This is further emphasised by his right foot, which is raised and crosses the skirt of the female figure. This seems to illustrate the state of play so to speak. In contrast to the pictures of the dancers Figure 9.1 and Figure 9.2, the female figure is on the left and male on the right. It seems that perhaps some transformation is taking place indicated by this change in the position of the couple. Perhaps this is an inner world change, but one which is also a reflection of aspects of the transference at this time.

In some of Harry's later pictures (not shown here) the dancers are shown in different relationships to each other again changing sides (Schaverien, 1991). The last of these dancer pictures is included as Figure 9.11 (see next page). This appears to be a marriage.

The last figure from the *Rosarium* is an androgynous figure which is called the alchemical marriage. Thus a similar resolution of aspects of Harry's inner world seems to be taking place here.

The point in this chapter has been to show how these stages emerged spontaneously in the pictures. But it has not been my aim merely to demonstrate that these processes occur; this is well known. Rather, my intention has been to demonstrate how the material manifestation of such inner images, in pictorial form, reflects the transference. Such pictures embody the desire of the analysand. The visual imagery is seductive and may evoke a corresponding countertransference. This needs to be recognised as a significant countertransference, evoked by the person of the analysand, but in conjunction with the aesthetic quality of the pictures. This is the "aesthetic countertransference" (Schaverien, 1995).

Conclusion

The *Psychology of the Transference* shows us how Eros in all its many manifestations is a guide to life in the therapeutic relationship. This is the main point of the somewhat arcane alchemical imagery. The relevance of this imagery is less immediately clear for the female analyst when working with women analysands. The heterosexual metaphor does not immediately seem to represent intercourse in the same gender pair and yet similar processes occur. Thus, too fixed a view of gender or of sexual orientation limits the possibilities for understanding offered by this text.

I hope to have demonstrated one of the ways in which pictures in analysis can seduce the analyst and shown that this may be of benefit to the analysand. Many of the people who come

Figure 9.11 The Marriage

for analysis lack the ability to seduce other people in any sense. Thus, to be able to "draw" the analyst "in" through the pictures they make may well be of positive benefit. It may be helpful to view internal images in some external form, but the relationship is also essential. Through this engagement the analysand's desire is transformed to psyche. The analysand may experience a relationship without demands and observe the patterns which are thus evoked. Eventually this leads to the integration and internalisation of the projected affect.

The pictures that I have shown correspond, in remarkable detail, to the processes which Jung describes, but this does not preclude other frames of reference for understanding the pictures or the therapeutic relationship. Certainly infantile processes were operating in the transference. Whilst developmental stages cannot be ignored, I propose that this is not always the main focus of the work; it is one element in the wider context of the unconscious material, both personal and collective. The incest desire can be understood as a literal wish to regress, but it can also be understood as a natural desire for individuation and rebirth (Jung, 1956). Both of these desires are operating simultaneously and to focus solely on one may be to miss seeing the other.

Acknowledgements

A version of this chapter was first published in *Inscape,* Winter edition, 1990. The illustrations were first published in *The Revealing Image* (1991) and are gratefully reprinted with permission from the publishers, Routledge.

References

Bion, W.R. (1970) *Attention and Interpretation,* London: Maresfield

Edinger, E. (1985) *The Anatomy of the Psyche: Alchemical Symbolism in Psychotherapy,* LaSalle Illinois: Open Court

Freud, S. (1912) "The Dynamics of Transference", in SE Vol. XII, Hogarth Press

Freud, S. (1915) "Observations on Transference Love", in SE Vol. XII, Hogarth Press

Jaccoby, M. (1984) *The Analytic Encounter,* Toronto: Inner City Books

Jung, C.G. (1946) *The Psychology of the Transference,* CW 16, Part II, Princeton: Bollingen.

Jung, C.G. (1953) *Psychology and Alchemy* CW 12, Part II, Princeton: Bollingen.

Jung, C.G. (1956) *Symbols of Transformation* CW 5, Part II, Princeton: Bollingen.

Jung, C.G. (1959) *Aion* CW 9, Part II, Princeton: Bollingen.

Hillman, J. (1972) *The Myth of Analysis,* New York: Harper Torch

Kant, I. (1790) *The Critique of Judgement,* translated by J. Creed Meredith, Oxford: Clarendon Press (1980)

Langer, S. (1967) *Feeling and Form,* London: Routledge and Kegan Paul

Samuels, A. (1985) *Jung and the Post-Jungians,* London and New York: Routledge and Kegan Paul

Samuels, A. (1989) *The Plural Psyche,* London and New York: Routledge

Schaverien, J. (1987) The scapegoat and the talisman: transference in art therapy; in *Images of Art Therapy*, Eds. Dalley, T., Case, C., Schaverien, J., Weir, F., Halliday, D., Nowell Hall, P., Waller, D. London: Tavistock

Schaverien, J. (1991) *The Revealing Image: Analytical Art Psychotherapy in Theory and Practice,* London & Philadelphia: Jessica Kingsley Publishers (this new edition 1999)

Schaverien, J. (1995) *Desire and the Female Therapist: Engendered Gazes in Psychotherapy and Art Therapy,* London and New York: Routledge

Schaverien, J. (1998) Art within the analytic relationship: scapegoat and transformation, paper for the *International Congress for Analytical Psychology* in August.

Schwartz-Salant, N. (1989) *The Borderline Personality: Vision and Healing,* Wilmette Illinois: Chiron

Sedgwick, D. (1994) *The Wounded Healer: Countertransference from a Jungian Perspective,* London and New York: Routledge

Stein, R. (1974) *Incest and Human Love,* Baltimore: Penguin [new edition (1998) entitled *The Betrayal of the Soul in Psychotherapy,* Woodstock: Spring]

10

Symbols and Transformation – The Meaning of Symbols within the Analytical Process

by Paul Brutsche

Symbols play an essential role in psychotherapy. They are so much part of therapy that for the process to have any effect, i.e., for an analysis to be successful, the client must be able to relate to a symbolic dimension. If somebody is not able to use their fantasy, to work playfully with the therapist at discovering possible meanings to the events in their life or to trust and honour the unconscious and their dreams, then one may consider it doubtful that the therapy will have any effect. Counselling and a reorientation may be possible, the client may receive encouragement and support, but if the feeling for the symbolic dimension is missing, in the end no real change will occur. A *conditio sine qua non* of a genuine personality transformation and of a genuine process of change is the analysand's ability to be open towards the symbolic dimension.

Every child has the ability to think symbolically. Yet many people seem to lose at least part of this ability, and for various reasons. Generally speaking, people stop thinking symbolically because they give priority to logical abstract thinking.

Part I: Symbolic Consciousness

I would like to first differentiate and describe two attitudes: the rational one and the symbolic one.

First the rational attitude:

1. This is the attitude that we see when, for instance, an analysand expects analysis to bring healing through the clear diagnosis of a psychic disturbance as a disease, whereupon adequate

measures can be applied. The core of the treatment may be described as follows: a clear terminology can be applied to an objective disease, which exists as such and independently from the individual, and the required steps can then be taken to eliminate it.

Some people do not really know what analysis is about and because of that, they automatically apply a model that they are familiar with, that of medical treatment. Yet they are not the only ones who believe that the "knowledgeable specialist" can give the right name to the disturbance and, by so doing, charm it away, as if words were endowed with a magical power. I have seen very differentiated people who know a lot about psychotherapy and who hold the same kind of belief. They may formulate a self-diagnosis, using their talent with words and many specialized terms. They do this very well but this "psychological approach" does not help them: it does not elucidate the problems and it does not free them; on the contrary, it makes them feel unsure and anxious. It is also obvious that this approach does not contribute to genuine psychic development and change, quite the opposite: sticking to rational concepts makes any transformation impossible.

2. Another form of rational attitude is that of the analysand who instinctively expects the treatment to be a "one-man show". By that, I mean that the therapist is considered to be a specialist armed with knowledge and competence who will sit across from a patient who becomes the object of his efforts and the receiver of his knowledge. There is no genuine interaction and no exchange between patient and therapist. The roles have been clearly and one-sidedly distributed: the therapist is the knowledgeable specialist and the analysand the unknowing receiver of the treatment.

This vertical model, including an unequal interaction between doctor and patient, is also the expression of a rationalist perception of the treatment as the application of knowledge which one – the specialist – has acquired through training and experience and the other – the analysand – does not possess, but to whom it is applied. There is no question of an exchange or of a common process.

Again, people who are quite independent thinkers may adopt this attitude – and not only less differentiated clients. Except that in such cases the specialist figure with superior knowledge may not be transferred onto the therapist, but rather be experienced as an inner instance that will appear in dreams, for example, as a lofty animus figure. This inner figure will clearly have super-ego characteristics: it presents high demands to the individual, making him/her feel inadequate. In this form, the rationalist worldly spirit takes possession of a person by continually demanding a self-development that may be achieved through more consciousness and a constantly increasing self-knowledge. Yet, psychic development requires a symbolic experience and not rational knowledge.

3. Rationalism may take on another form, that of causal explanations. In this perspective psychic problems have a cause that is to be found in the analysand's past, i.e., in an unfavourable family constellation. According to this cause-and-effect type of thinking, a

childhood constellation has provoked a disturbance that is still influencing the client's present life. It is possible to eliminate it by becoming conscious of its causes.

It may well be that this therapeutic "fix-it" model is not applied as crudely as I am describing it; yet it is often present in the background. The reductive approach (as Jung calls it), i.e., an approach focused on causes and on childhood biographies, is essentially based on rational thinking. It is a one-dimensional and linear, causal type of thinking. It considers psychic phenomena to be products of objective, past facts.

Reductive explanations are not only at the core of some therapeutic models; they are also part of the way some analysands think. And as such they truly hinder psychic transformation: the analysand cannot get away from mentally reconstructing his biography and, although this may give him a certain intellectual satisfaction, it contributes little to his psychic evolution.

4. Finally, a rational attitude is characterized by the fact that it follows the logic of abstract thinking. Logical thinking uses either / or categories. This makes it quite adequate in the field of natural sciences, but not in relation to grasping the reality of the psyche. This intellectual way of thinking makes it impossible for many people to relate to the depth of their psyche and to symbolical experience. They remain trapped in trying to see things literally, to categorize them and to describe causal relationships.

As far as analysis goes, it is not always the so-called "thinking types" who fall prey to a rational attitude. People with another typology may have the same tendency, since the fascination of logical thinking has more to do with rationalism than with genuine thinking.

And now a few ideas concerning symbolic thinking.

I would like to demonstrate the characteristic of a symbolic approach by presenting a dream. The dreamer is a 50 year-old woman with an above-average talent for languages; she works as a teacher. She has had analysis twice before, with other therapists, and would like to start a new analysis because over many years, she has written numerous poems and texts without daring to have them published. She has the feeling of being completely blocked in relation to showing her writings to others and would like to find relief.

The dream was told as follows:

I am sitting on a full train, together with a number of psychologists who are coming back from a congress (about group psychology) that has just finished. A therapist I know (Brutsche?) is among them; he is sitting across from me. An unknown couple, a man and a woman come in and take a seat not far from me. They have obviously just had a very powerful experience – maybe they have just had a violent fight – in any case something one does not experience every day, a kind of extreme thing. Brutsche (?) talks to them, mentioning a cantata by Johann Sebastian Bach. It makes them both cry. Then I start talking, reminding them of a poem by Hölderlin and of a specific verse: … "You (Gods) above us …" ["Ihr (Götter) da oben."] This makes them cry again. Now they are holding hands.

How should we understand the dream? Obviously, a congress about group psychology has just come to an end. Now something healing is taking place, just there on a train where analyst and analysand happen to meet. They are both in the same situation and they meet an unknown couple.

The congress is finished, the meeting during which specialized knowledge is exchanged, formulated in specialized lingo. In reality, the analysand often organizes "mental congresses" that take place in her brain and during which psychological themes are debated. During these, she sees herself as a helpless case. Obviously – and that is good – this psychological "shop talk" has come to an end; she seems to be over it. She does not think about herself so much any more, she no longer reflects herself psychologically from the point of view of the group and of the observer. She is no longer characterized only by her symptoms.

What is also new is that the analyst has become a human being, who has stopped barricading himself in the ivory tower of his hermetic knowledge and moves around the world of ordinary people. A new image of the inner analyst has thus appeared, who no longer functions as a dominating super-ego; rather, his human presence has become a healing factor.

The problem that seems to be described is represented by the couple that has just had an argument. It is an unknown couple: we may assume that it represents a general problem that is still unknown to the analysand. They sit close to her – the problem is becoming more pressing, the analysand must pay attention. It is a problem that has to do with a split, with a dramatic lack of unity or, to use the image in the dream, with an unbridgeable conflict between a man and a woman, between the masculine and the feminine. This seems to be the dreamer's personal problem, but it also has a more global meaning: that of a lack of co-operation between the opposites, of the way they are in conflict. This leads to an antagonism between thinking and feeling, spirit and soma, reason and instinct, or rational and materialist attitudes.

It is in fact the case that these poles are quite separate in this woman's psyche. This dia-bolic state, i.e., this non-symbolical being, this lack of oneness with oneself is also quite typical of our time. It is a theme that concerns many people and the dreamer is confronted with it "on the train of our time". It may be described briefly with expressions such as "lack of soul" and "lack of relatedness".

The healing does not seem to come from some clever psychological interpretation. This would only satisfy the intellect and create a larger distance between the poles that have to be brought closer to each other.

Rather, the inner analyst mentions a Bach cantata and this provokes liberating tears. He is actually talking about something that expresses a general human experience in poetic and musical form. And the analysand does the same by mentioning a poem by Hölderlin, that speaks of a transcendental dimension: "You (Gods) above us … ". The spirit to which she refers, and which in this case has healing power, is the spirit of artistic expression through music and poetry. It is imagination and fantasy that are able to give a higher meaning to what is just "being". Here, a creative and inspiring spirit takes the place of an intellectual spirit, of a kind of disillusioned thinking. This artistic spirit thinks in symbols and creates symbols and this establishes a connection with "superior" factors, with the archetypes. It is this spirit that has healing power. It heals by reconnecting the opposites and by allowing pain and feelings to be expressed. On the other hand, the rational attitude that we have discussed before does not heal. It is not able to "save", i.e., to make whole again and to connect to something greater. The rational attitude forms structures according to the categories of scientific reflection. This deprives it of the transforming potential that is specific to symbolic thinking. When someone thinks symbolically, they use more than their intellect: they are touched emotionally and this brings a new psychic experience that provokes a change.

Indeed, this dream shows beautifully the various aspects that are specific to symbolic knowledge. Let me summarize these aspects:

Perceiving symbolically involves seeing *in images*, understanding with *one's feelings*, becoming *intuitively* aware and reaching an *integral* form of awareness (of consciousness).

These specific characteristics give symbolic perception the power to heal the soul. It is a kind of perception that is adapted to the nature of the psyche. And this means that it is a perception that activates the transformative potential contained (only) in the psyche.

Part II: Symbolic Reality

Let us come to the second part of this paper, in which I would like to look at "symbolic *reality*" – as opposed to "symbolic *consciousness*", which I wrote about in the first part.

Analysis often makes people experience for the first time the existence of a symbolic reality parallel to the concrete, material reality. Whether one starts believing that something in oneself is really beginning to change, or whether one is convinced that everything will always remain the same, depends on discovering this inner symbolic reality. This discovery may also allow the person to feel psychically alive instead of living in an atmosphere of deadly boredom.

Some people seem to be caught in a kind of earthly concretism. For them, there is only one reality, that of the world around them. They lose contact with the reality of their own person or continually push it aside.

Let me describe a few of the forms that this strange self-denial, or if you prefer, this dependency on the outer world may take.

Some people are totally identified with their social persona. For them, criteria such as prestige, social status, the image of a perfect family with, for instance, well brought-up children and academic careers – these and other signs of achievement and success play a central role. The value of the individual is then defined by his image. By image, I mean physical appearance, social status and professional position, all of these being measured against the official standards defining what makes a person successful. An existence that is defined in such a collective manner is collective, but is also governed by much too concrete aspects. One forgets that the individual exists as an inner personality, quite independently from official norms and visible prestigious values.

It can also happen that people forget themselves in relationships. I am thinking for instance of the overcaring mother who finds meaning only in her child, or of the analysand who never stops talking about her husband. These people lose a large part of their relationship to themselves because relationships to significant others take up too much space. This is a symptom of a lack of feeling for the inner psyche and for symbolic reality.

Outer factors may also be overvalued when people attribute too much importance to somatic aspects, or see these as some kind of absolute value. This may be seen in couples for which the relationship is reduced to sexuality; or it can be expressed in a tendency to always consider psychic problems as having a physiological cause.

The transfer of psychic reality onto an outer, objective world, or to the level of relationships, or of the body, can also happen in yet another way: some people make one concrete task into the absolute centre of their life.

The four attitudes above have in common the fact that, in the last resort, only *one* reality is considered valuable: that of the concrete, outer, collective world. At the same time, they attribute too little value to another side – the symbolic, inner, individual reality of the soul.

Analysis actually aims at discovering that, beside the reality of concrete things, there is also a symbolic reality, that of imagination and – given that the psyche essentially expresses itself in images and fantasies – of the contact with psychic reality through experiencing one's own fantasy.

I would like to present another dream that will help us see again the aspects that are specific to symbolic reality.

The dreamer is a 40 year-old woman, who works as a teacher and lives with a journalist. She suffers from a lack of genuine relationships, both to her present partner and to her family.

Here is the dream:

My partner drops in where I live. He is in a great hurry because he has some business to take care of with his brother. He has no time for me.

In the afternoon I meet a man in a restaurant with whom I spontaneously get on very well. We have an intimate relationship, i.e., surprisingly enough we share an erotic experience in this neutral place.

I then have to go to a public conference, during which my partner will give a paper. Numerous elegantly dressed, famous people are there.

Apart from my partner I have an official lover. Both are asking me to choose one of them.

The unknown man whom I met in the afternoon shows up again. I go for a walk with him. I describe my situation to him, i.e., the situation of my two partners. While I am talking I realize that I have to decide for myself and not for one or the other man.

This is the dream – what does it show us? It shows us a dreamer who has relationships with two different kinds of partners. One is connected to her actual life-partner and to a kind of official lover, the other to a lover whom she did not know until then and with whom she experiences an intimate contact.

These two types of men represent two different attitudes that are present in the woman's psyche. There is a man in her who, like her partner in the dream, is very busy with concrete things that are considered to have absolute priority. It is a kind of mono-manic obsession with objectives and concrete objects. The relationship to the dream ego, i.e., the relationship to the dreamer's own person seems to be of secondary importance. The partner's attitude in the dream looks like an animus possession towards which the dreamer is helpless. Because the energy is invested in achieving concrete things, the dreamer's ego does not get what she needs. It is being pushed into the background and forgotten, because objects, objectives and achievements have absolute priority.

An official lover is there to console the frustrated ego. In reality, his function is probably to provide moments of pleasurable satisfaction that will compensate the frustration arising from the dreamer's obsession with the objective world. This compensation, this making-up to the forgotten ego may take various forms: she may give herself a treat, buy herself something or allow herself from time to time to do something that she enjoys. This is in general how "the official lover" consoles a neglected ego, offering a compensatory gesture. For a short time the ego gets what it needs, but not in a way that would be appropriate for the psyche: the ego just satisfies a greedy instinct.

Yet, the dream shows that another attitude would be possible. It is still unclear what this would be – but it is represented by the unknown man whom she meets in the afternoon in a neutral place, in a restaurant.

This man concentrates entirely on the dreamer. It seems that a complex process of finding oneself in the other is taking place. This provides the ego with a deep feeling of acceptance and closeness, accompanied by an overwhelming experience of inner satisfaction.

In this sense, the man seems to represent an attitude that the dreamer still has to discover, an attitude that is focused on herself as a subject with lovable, valuable and unique characteristics.

I find it typical that the meeting with the unknown man who will relate to the dream ego takes place "in the afternoon", i.e., in the afternoon of life, after mid-life. I also find it interesting that this meeting would take place "in a neutral place" and "in a restaurant". The "neutral" aspect could mean that for this encounter to take place, the outer world first has to be "neutralized" – this will allow a subjective reality to be perceived.

What is more, according to the dream the encounter takes place in a restaurant, in a place where people meet, where they eat outside their home, maybe together with friends on a special occasion. We could see this to mean that taking care of oneself, meeting with one's being cannot be a solipsistic self-reflection; it is a process that must take place in the broader context of human encounter. Here a world of communion and communication takes the place of the world of things and provides food for the soul. The person who is contained in this world feels that she is more than a thing. She experiences herself as a communicative *ens symbolicum*, as a symbolic person living from exchanges with others.

The dream then describes the partner's activity: he is "giving a paper in front of a group of elegantly dressed people". This could mean that, when focussing on the outer world, the dreamer has a tendency to (want to) impress others with words. This kind of self-representation does not really help the ego express itself. It is not the subject in the dreamer who is heard, but her partner. The dreamer herself is forced into the role of the passive listener, who has to accept elegant ideas that have been formulated by someone else.

The partner and the official lover are jealous of each other and demand that the dreamer choose one of them. She should make a decision. This shows how powerful this objective perception of reality is and how ambivalent it can make people – there is an ambivalence between pure achievement and addiction to pleasure, but also between being guided by absolute norms or being driven by basic instincts.

The unknown man, on the other hand, does not provoke an either / or situation. He does not make absolute demands at the expense of the ego. In the woman's quest he represents the present and a "thou". By speaking with him, she understands some things better. In this sense, this man represents another perception of reality, a perception that takes into account the reality of the subject and serves as an inner mirror for conscious reflection. This means that he also stands for an inner psychic reality that is capable of understanding and working through the subject's experience: the ability to create images, fantasies and to imagine, through which one may step back and perceive things symbolically. What we are seeing here is an underlying ability to perceive symbolically the experience created by the individual, as opposed to a simple "functioning" in accordance with objective and collective norms.

The dream suggests that the analysand needs this type of transformation of her basic attitude. It is a psychic challenge that everyone must face. People, no matter who they are, must find the means to relate to an inner psychic reality. They must experience imagination and symbolic perception as something real and dynamic.

We may ask what is the role of analysis in this process of moving away from the world of objects and ready-made opinions and into a world of individual perception? In analysis, we encourage people not to look at things in the way that they think they should be looked at. We try to help them take into account their personal reactions and feelings and to trust what is expressed through fantasies and images. In this sense, we reinforce a symbolic reality and create a space in which psychic reality may develop.

Symbolic reality can only manifest itself if I turn towards myself. This happens with somebody else's support, i.e., through the analyst showing interest in my inner world. In this atmosphere of empathy – and only then – I start feeling sure that I do not simply function in an unidimensional, outer reality, but also have in me a psychic reality that deserves respect and that is just as valid.

Part III: The Reality of Symbols

I would like to draw attention to a third aspect, that of the process through which symbols bring about a transformation. We have talked about a symbolic form of consciousness and about the reality of symbolic imagination. What I have in mind now is to show how, in itself, working with symbols brings a transformation. Symbols contain a specific potential for change and transformation. Here, I am thinking of dreams, of paintings, of spontaneous fantasies or of active imagination. All this material from the unconscious has effects, and these effects bring about a transformation.

Let me go into more detail about the following two aspects: the effective properties of symbols and their transformative potential. Firstly, what kind of effects do symbols have? I see four different dimensions:

1. Symbols are images that provoke a reaction.

It is actually amazing how symbols may stir us, "move" us, due precisely to their expressing things in images. Suppose, for instance, that an analyst were able to translate the meaning of a dream into abstract words and to communicate these ideas to the analysand, as plain ideas and without the "flesh" of images. The effect would never be the same as that of the direct and durable "insight" – in the sense of a "just so feeling" – provided by the imaginary language of the dream. A young analysand told me recently how surprised he was that dreams could have such strong effects. Yet, he was not talking about the efforts we had made together to start understanding his dreams. What he was referring to were the images in the dreams, and not our common reflection. He was quite right of course, and every analyst knows that it is only after symbolic material has come up that this other dimension starts working, leading the process from the thin air of rational reflection into a deeply emotional experience. An insight that is not supported by an image does not stimulate movement and so does not transform anything. Symbols, on the other hand, present what is to be grasped in an imaginary form and they are thus able to touch the person emotionally and to bring a transformation.

2. Symbols have a meaning that surprises.

We cannot help but be constantly surprised at how accurately dreams represent psychic situations. It is very impressive to see that dreams are not just the "garbage bin" into which leftovers from the day are thrown out. They are original, or even brilliant, compilations of people's experiences. It seems clear to me that they are staged by an incredibly inventive director, or rather author, who in addressing his own messages to consciousness shows a tremendous talent for synthesis, description, comparison, etc., in short for artistic expression. The experience that something behind the symbolic material has its own way of thinking has, by itself, this kind of effect, even before one understands what idea is being expressed. It thus makes sense to accept that another kind of spirit is at work, thinking beside one's own consciousness. In itself, this aspect has tremendous effects.

3. Symbols use an elementary language that provokes an emotional reaction.

It seems that symbols are also always addressed to the archaic being who still lives in us. They activate a more natural, more primitive and more genuine side in us. And apparently they resonate to something of the past, that has to do with the experience of the child and with that of archaic humankind. This elementary dimension – both archaic and historical – is always present in symbols and it has a very intense effect. This is what always happens when we reconnect with the forgotten child, or our lost archaic side, and listen to what they have to say.

4. Symbols have an effect because their curious nature fascinates us.

A French philosopher wrote: *Le symbole est quelque chose qui donne à penser"* (the symbol is something that makes one think). Symbolic contents provoke our curiosity because they really seem ungraspable. They invite us to be open to a hidden meaning. This mysterious, sublime character of the symbol refers to a higher level, but it can of course also be misused. It is easy to find examples of this in recent history, where some political regimes have surrounded themselves with specific ideologies and images, in order to exploit the numinous effect of symbols. Yet, as far as analysis is concerned, we can say that this fascinating effect of symbols is very important in the sense that if they succeed in fascinating consciousness, they will also help the ego focus less on immediate gratification and more on spiritual objectives.

In summary, we may say that given their formal characteristics, symbols have effects through the mere fact that they are there: their imaginal quality provokes a reaction, their hidden meaning astounds us, their elementary nature impresses us and their sublime aspects fascinate us.

This multidimensional quality frees ego consciousness from being grounded in itself, i.e., it makes it aware that something greater than the ego exists and has effects on consciousness. The ego is thus encouraged to join in play with a high-spirited, almost Dionysian spirit expressing itself by touching all the various senses.

Part IV: Transformation through Symbols

Let us now see what we mean by "transformation" in relation to symbols. What kind of transformation is it? Here again we need to differentiate. I cannot help it, but because of my Jungian psyche I have to distinguish among four aspects!

1. The transformation that is provoked by symbols is, first of all, a result of the fundamental experience of the ego being part of a larger psychic reality.

Through this experience the person learns that an inner world exists, that is just as big and just as real as the outer world. This inner world reaches beyond the ego and the ego comes to know this. For instance, dreams use very old memories from the dreamer's past or they bring aspects from outside the person's own life, showing themes and situations borrowed from the context of earlier epochs. The borders of the limited ego world are crossed, there is a return to the past, to the personal history of the dreamer but also to a collective history; there may also be elements belonging to the future. As we all know, symbolic products from the unconscious are not limited by spatial boundaries either: they are thus situated outside of both time and space.

This "timeless" and "spaceless" quality is characteristic of symbolic material and, by affecting ego perception, it has a transformative potential. The ego then understands that it is not isolated in the present and in an arbitrary part of the cosmos – it feels connected with time and history, with the world and with the human race. The encounter with symbols and the work on their contents bring an experience of something that otherwise would remain a philosophical concept: the discovery that one can feel contained, as an individual, in a greater psychic reality and that one may be carried by this entity. This actually corresponds to an important change in relation to the ego's "normal" attitude. The ego usually sees itself only within the time and space limits defined by consciousness and only within a monadic type of reality. Through working with dreams, people may discover that the ego that they had taken for granted is linked to a greater reality. This allows a gradual change to take place, in a process that will lead to a completely new situation, that of an individual who knows that he is contained in a greater cosmos providing security, or if you want, salvation – an individual who has thus experienced a healing power.

2. Another type of transformation brought about by symbols has to do with their enlarging the perception that the ego has of itself and even turning it upside down.

Every individual has a certain self-image, according to which he tries to live. The symbolic material provided by the unconscious shows him that this image is not – or no longer – adequate, or that he also lives in a way that is very different from what his self-image would dictate. In this sense, again ego consciousness is freed from too narrow a perception that is linked to its self-image. It is confronted with other aspects of the personality, with other ways of thinking or with as yet unknown possibilities.

Here again, something is "put upside down", i.e., transformed. This kind of change is connected to a *videatur et altera pars*, to a revolutionary step in which things are perceived from an Archemedean point situated outside ego-consciousness. The perspective suggested by this kind of view is not only new in the sense that it modifies the person's self-image, it is also different because it aims for a wholeness and renewal that are foreign to the ego. By nature, the ego focuses on things and, as a result, it is interested only in personal, idiosyncratic aspects. It is also typically possessive and would rather keep to what it knows; the ego thus resists change.

The symbolic material introduces the ego to another side of reality, to other aspects of the person, and this enables it to constantly revise its self-image and to adapt it to changing life circumstances. In this sense we may say that symbols are the "motors" of a permanent psychic revolution. This process of transformation must continually take place for a person to be psychically healthy. Symbols help the individual fulfil this prerequisite, because they connect ego-consciousness with a larger dimension of psychic evolution – something that the ego is not able to do because of the above-mentioned tendency to resist change.

3. Symbols also have transformational effects because they unite the opposites and are aimed towards a greater wholeness.

Ego-consciousness – which we must also take into account – necessarily tends to differentiate and to separate. It classifies according to categories: spatial categories (up-down, left-right), time categories (now-later, today-yesterday), but also according to moral criteria (good-evil) and to emotional reactions (pleasant-unpleasant, adequate-not adequate). The ego needs this differentiating in order to orientate itself in the concrete sense of the word, i.e., to find its way in concrete time and space, but also to know where it stands, psychically and spiritually, in relation to life. Yet constantly classifying things also tends to have negative consequences: blockages and one-sidedness, which gradually form a procrustean bed around the soul and prevent it from breathing and from moving. I am thinking, for instance, of convictions, values, ideals and religious attitudes that are no longer the expression of a psychic truth that make the individual feel alive and that have become formulas, routines or obsessions.

One characteristic of symbols is that they reconnect the psyche to incompatible aspects that the ego would have, out of need, repressed. One cannot expect the ego to adopt a position while at the same time declaring itself favourable to its opposite. It is thus only natural that its attitude will be one-sided and pedantic.

In bringing into play subversive material, symbols bring a transformation in the sense of a moral conversion. They do not do this to make the ego feel insecure or to undermine its position. They do it to help the psyche find a better relationship to a more basic reality, i.e., to the reality of the self. It is the self's nature and vitality that are being expressed whenever new connections are established between apparently irreconcilable opposites, whenever a *conjunctio oppositorum* takes place. All these instances when the opposites are being overcome and transcended add up to form what Jung calls the individuation process.

Without symbols this process of confrontation *with* the opposites and of *mediation* between the opposites would remain theoretical. With them, it becomes a genuine experience. Dreams bring into play the shadow and evil and thus necessarily lead the individual to reconsider the ideology that has guided his life. For instance, they may move an atheist to overcome his resistance towards accepting that he also has to confront supernatural aspects. Or they may show the believer that something in his image of God is no longer adequate.

Although the ego would not be able to initiate the process spontaneously, we know that this kind of transformation is no "spiritual luxury". It is also not arbitrary and it corresponds to a psychic need. The point is that, in order to remain psychically healthy, we need to stay in step with the changing ways in which the self aims to realize itself in our life and in our beliefs.

4. And finally, the transformation mediated by symbols has a fourth dimension: symbols are a bridge to new things, to what we are not yet familiar with.

The alchemists say: *Habentibus symbolum facile est transitus*, those who have a symbol find it easy to make the passage. We also know that Jung considered this anticipatory component of the symbol to be extremely important. He writes that the symbol is " … the best possible expression for a complex fact not yet clearly apprehended by consciousness" (1954). As far as the creative function of the symbol goes, i.e., as far as its function as a future-oriented mediator and midwife goes, we may remember that from a historical point of view, it was always in the world of the arts – that is in a world in which symbols play a central role – that the ground for new tendencies and for new times was prepared.

Concerning analysis, we can also show that the symbols appearing in dreams etc. have a teleological quality. It may be hard for us to accept that we are not able to see into the future. Specialists try to use statistics to predict the evolution of the economy and, sometimes, a prophet may be able to predict the future without using a computer. But basically, we are trapped in the present, our consciousness does not reach into the future.

Yet, the psyche is able to reach beyond present consciousness. Dreams may speak of things that, until then, had not occurred to us. Or they may use images in which something new is taking shape, at a non-verbal level and long before consciousness understands what they are about. The power that is creating, and the images that have been created, make it possible for us to grasp something that we are not yet able to understand and to consciously analyse. Yet, this something may move us to broaden the field of our conscious perception and to turn our antenna in a specific direction, until we start understanding. It is as if magnets were being placed in the field of what we do not know, that will attract the ego away from what it knows.

It seems clear to me that the process, through which the symbols exert a force of attraction from within the field of the unknown, brings an absolute change, and that it is at this level that their transformational potential is to be found. The ego is not able to initiate this process, since it cannot spontaneously have totally new ideas. It can only become creative if the unconscious expresses itself through the symbols, opening new channels towards the unknown. What is more, the ego is absolutely unable to foresee its own personal development.

Yet, the ego needs this kind of opening to the future. Also it needs these impulses to be formulated in terms that feel like a genuine expression of the psyche – and not like a pure invention. Without the psychic evolutionary potential that is contained in the symbol, the individual would remain blocked. These blockages may take the form of "home-made" self-healing strategies, or they may manifest in psychosomatic symptoms. Mental and psychophysical health is not possible if psychic life does not evolve and does not change to include new elements. However, this forward movement should not be guided by illusionary programmes; it should be grounded in genuine transformational impulses that come from the individual soul. The symbols indicate what the psyche wants and they show the unexpected, illogical and non-linear path along which this renewal can take place.

This will be my conclusion: Symbols are the pathfinders in the quest for constant renewal. They are also the companions of an ego that is continuously reaching beyond itself and thus constantly changing.

References

Jung, C.G. (1954) The Transcendent Function § 148 in *The Structure and Dynamics of the Psyche*, The Collected Works vol. 8.

11

Learning from Images

by Michael Edwards

Susan Bach will be best remembered for her remarkable observations about spontaneously produced pictures made by organically ill patients in clinical settings. Her early intuitive interpretive skills soon developed into a structured and systematic series of perceptions, which enabled her to record and even to predict the progress of life-threatening physical illnesses solely from the evidence of elements in the drawings and paintings. Many of these were by seriously ill children. In 1990 she published a comprehensive illustrated account of her life's work: *Life Paints Its Own Span: On the Significance of Spontaneous Pictures by Severely Ill Children*. While ready to acknowledge a limited direct therapeutic role for the making of such pictures in the context of organic illness, I think it would be fair to say that her main interest was not in "art as therapy" as it is generally understood, but in diagnostic and prognostic information which could be deduced from patients' pictures and then used to clinical advantage. This meant she developed a key role in influencing medical decisions, sometimes leading to revising earlier diagnoses or changing treatment plans. Perhaps it is also significant that she worked for three years at Netherne Hospital, where early pioneering work in art therapy was closely linked to a psychiatric medical model. However, she makes clear in her writing that she was indebted to C.G. Jung for insights into the psyche-soma relation and the idea of treating the patient as a whole person.

   With these thoughts in mind and from the very different perspective of Jungian art therapy as it is generally practised, there is a conceptual threshold to be negotiated. A reading of Susan Bach's published work suggests her research taught her to recognize that the unconscious "knew" things at the very deep psycho-physical level we might understand as *knowledge by the body*. In many of the cases she reviewed throughout her professional life the pictures relate to an irreversible organic condition. In such cases her insights could be prognostic with remarkable accuracy in revealing how much time remained for the patient to live. She called this "inner knowingness" and from it she was able to perceive hitherto unknown diagnostic information simply from a picture made by that patient. Where she had no knowledge of the person she would ask for details of age, sex and any known colour blindness. Amongst other variables, the representation of colour and number were given considerable importance.

The pictures were collected by her and catalogued systematically. Thus they were not usually seen as belonging to the patients who made them, but as clinical material, much like X-ray or scan photographs. In medical terms, the study of the pictures had obvious implications for treatment, and more generally for how to provide the most appropriate caring environment for the patient, the parents and others involved. Sensitive pastoral counselling would include facing up to the truth of the situation. From the emotional point of view much of Susan Bach's work can be seen as recognizing *unconscious mourning* in the pictures in anticipation of an inevitable premature death. The mourning process is both by and for the patient. She found that this can be expressed through a patient's pictures, without necessarily registering consciously. For the most part, she does not choose to speculate on the *experience* of expressing this inner situation pictorially, although in her last paper, *Small Circles – Closed Early: On the Stories behind Dying Children's Pictures; A Contribution to their Evaluation* (see chapter 1), she turns her attention to verbal and written responses by patients about their own pictures. In recognizing here the importance of language as an additional source of insight into the patient's imagery she moves towards a more patient-centred approach.[1]

Most art therapists work with a similar hypothesis of unconscious perception. Many have also been influenced by Jung's insights into the "complementary" function of the unconscious in relation to consciousness. Furthermore, it is not unusual for an art therapist to help a client work through a period of mourning in which the unconscious is quite clearly playing a part through pictorial representation. On the other hand, it would be unusual for an art therapist to rely heavily upon interpretive skills alone, especially "blind", without direct knowledge of the patient. This knowledge would usually be of the *emotional* life of the patient, which in a strictly medical context might normally receive less detailed attention. Susan Bach's work has to be seen as something of a special category. Thus, while she showed great clarity and conviction in her insights, this usually, it seems, meant a narrower focus and more reductive style of interpretation than might be used by most art therapists. Her findings were of course based upon extensive research and clinical experience, mostly using medical models of physical illness. However, she was familiar with the psychotherapeutic potential of "spontaneous art" in mental health situations. Her own experience of the art work of the mentally ill seems to have been mainly at Netherne Hospital, Surrey, where pioneering experiments in art therapy sought to combine the encouragement of undirected artistic expression by the patients, facilitated by Edward Adamson as "hospital artist", with psychiatric interpretation and evaluation of the results. She tells us also of her subsequent participation in a three-year study group at

---

[1] It was always part of the Zürich method to record the children's comments on a given picture. See chapter 2 by Hans-Peter Weber in *Life Paints Its Own Span* [Editor].

St. Bernard's Hospital, London which gathered the resources of psychiatrists, psychotherapists and "clinical artists" from ten mental hospitals. These early researches were influential upon her understanding and working methods (Bach, 1990).

Previously, her own Jungian analysis seems to have included some "spontaneous painting". Susan Bach acknowledges a debt to Jung, whom she met on several occasions and who confirmed her diagnosis of physical illness in a picture on at least one occasion (Bach, 1990, p. 75). From this background she is critical of rash or unskilled interpretations of pictures:

> To my great regret, misuse of spontaneous paintings and their interpretation is becoming more and more widespread. Some workers in the field mistake their own interpretation of a picture and its contents for what a patient has expressed and tend to project their own understanding and believe that this is the "message" contained therein.

One wonders which professional group of "workers in the field" she had in mind here. Art therapists are, of course, specifically and very carefully trained *not* to fall into this kind of projective trap, which can arise from unrecognized counter-transference issues or other subjective factors in the situation. There are important further considerations here. Pictures from the unconscious in particular tend to attract just such projections from lay observers, and no doubt to a certain extent from all of us. However, *art of all kinds attracts interpretation*, not just from the lay public who "know what they like", but also from various specialists whose expertise does not necessarily extend to a developed understanding of art itself. Thus anthropologists, historians, philosophers, politicians, psychologists, psychiatrists, sociologists, theologians, not to mention therapists and healers in many cultures from time to time express very serious views about images which may be informed more by the insights of their profession than by art historical or aesthetic considerations. Thus, while I share her concerns about inappropriate interpretations of pictures, the dividing line between this hazard and the apparently intuitive or even expert "reading" of a picture may be narrow. This must sometimes include interpretations made out of context by experts in other fields. This was caricatured by a cartoon in a professional paper some years ago in which two "psychiatrists" were shown visiting a modern art exhibition. Standing in front of an abstract work, one says to the other: "Should we call him in for observation?"

The joke relies upon a simplistic acceptance of the concept of diagnosing from pictures and that such a diagnosis carries the full weight of medical authority. It suggests implicitly that this undercuts whatever might be the views of art experts as to what the work represents and that *psychiatrists know more about artists from their art than artists know themselves.* What shocks about such an idea is that the change of context from gallery to clinic is disregarded. It is as if the language and values of art, the historic evolution of expression through imagery, is expected to assume a lower level of credibility than the psychiatric opinion. For similar reasons I experience a certain uneasiness about the following passage:

After decades of collecting, studying and evaluating spontaneous material, I was staggered to find that the main insights won from it into the total person, both his body and mind, are also applicable outside the clinical field, in our own everyday life situations, as well as in works of art. (Bach, 1990)

While I have little doubt that Susan Bach was an extremely gifted and intelligent interpreter of pictures, my misgivings are about trying to generalize too extensively from this knowledge. Even Jung fell into this kind of generalization on occasions, although he personally experienced the value of making pictures. As an amateur artist he made some competent landscapes around the turn of the century and subsequently of course he made many images "from the unconscious". However, when writing about Picasso in 1932 Jung unusually sounds wholly the traditional reductive psychiatrist, [1] even seeming to hide behind this as a screen:

For almost twenty years I have occupied myself with the psychology of pictorial representation of psychic happenings, and I am therefore in a position to look at Picasso's pictures from a professional point of view. On the basis of my experience, I can assure the reader that Picasso's *psychic problems*, insofar as they find expression in his work, are strictly analogous to those of my patients. Unfortunately I cannot offer proof on this point, as the comparative material is known only to a few specialists. (Jung, 1932/1966, p. 135 – emphasis mine)

Elsewhere Jung is frequently much more cautious and generous when talking about works of art, as in the following example written ten years earlier:

In order to do justice to a work of art, analytical psychology must rid itself entirely of medical prejudice; for a work of art is not a disease, and consequently requires a different approach from the medical one. (Jung, 1963)

There is more of traditional psychiatry than psychological curiosity in Jung's assessment of Picasso. The compensatory, prospective and creative aspects of the unconscious, to which Jung constantly drew attention elsewhere, are not considered here. In Jung's "pathologizing" of Picasso it is important to remember his frequent dictum that it is the *attitude* in relation to unconscious contents rather than the contents themselves which determines whether or not we are in the presence of a disturbed state of mind. It is a distinction to be made between visionary and psychotic experience. Since Picasso was not a patient and in fact was in social and cultural terms a highly successful individual, despite some of the eccentricities of genius, it hardly seems as if his psychic situation was strictly analogous to that of Jung's patients. On this occasion and despite his personal "confrontation with the unconscious", Jung's views about Picasso here seem inconsistent with the main body of his psychological understanding. When recollecting his own plunge into very disturbing imagery he writes:

---

[1] For a somewhat different viewpoint on Jung's aims in this brief essay, see Goldstein and Harborne in chapter 7 [Editor].

It is, of course, ironical that I, a psychiatrist, should at every step of my experiment have run into the same psychic material which is the stuff of psychosis and is found in the insane. This is the fund of unconscious images which fatally confuse the mental patient. But it is also the matrix of a mythopoetic imagination which has vanished from our rational age. (Jung, 1963)

Following the break with Freud in 1913, Jung's personal crisis led to a series of visionary pictures and writings in his journals and on the walls of his tower at Bollingen. In 1916, the year that Jung first encouraged his patients to make pictures from their dreams and fantasies, he set out some of his tentative ideas about giving expression to unconscious imagery and its possibilities for healing in *The Transcendent Function,* a paper which was not published until forty-one years later. In it he discusses the relation between "aesthetic" and "psychological" dimensions of images which arise spontaneously from the unconscious.

One tendency seems to be the regulating principle of the other; both are related in a compensatory manner. Experience confirms this formula. As far as it is possible at this stage to draw general conclusions, we would say that the tendency towards aesthetic expression seems to need the tendency towards understanding, and equally the tendency towards understanding needs that of aesthetic expression. (Jung, 1922)

By "understanding" in this context Jung appears to mean psychological insight, and by "aesthetic expression" a concern for the formal properties of the image. Without something of the former, he suggests, there is a risk of empty and meaningless formalism, and without aesthetic constraints of some kind the image may be raw, chaotic and uncontrolled. Besides writing *The Transcendent Function* and first encouraging his patients to follow his own example by making images from their dreams and fantasies, 1916 was also the year in which he first drew a spontaneous mandala, a recurring archetypal image that helped shape his understanding of the Collective Unconscious. While Jung, the psychologist, was formulating ideas about working *with* images from the unconscious as "Active Imagination", some artists and writers were turning directly to psychology for inspiration.

In the Arts at this time, Expressionism was an established but perhaps growing influence. Developing from nineteenth century Romanticism, it affirmed and encouraged the impact of individual emotion upon artistic style. Expressionism was an exploration of technique and style in the communication of affect. When Art Therapy emerged as an identifiable profession after the Second World War, it is not surprising that Expressionism became its first artistic role-model. The other main artistic influence upon art therapy, Surrealism, was innovative not so much in style as in *subject matter.* The Surrealists found inspiration in dreams and fantasies. Since the pictures and writings they made were concretized representations of this inner material, the process was not unlike Jung's "active imagination", in a Fine Art context.

Surrealism grew out of an earlier movement, *Dada,* founded by a group of French and German writers and artists. Dada was intended to provoke outrage and scandal. As well as being against war, the establishment, conventional morality and rationality, it was also *anti-art.*

By deliberately frustrating normal habits of perception, the Dadaists, like the Surrealists who succeeded them, forced attention inwards, thereby invoking the psyche. Its paradoxical effect, despite much that was apparently nihilistic or nonsensical, was to change art itself. Dada was a new Romanticism (Edwards, 1989). In their attempt to follow the psyche rather than artistic conventions they advocated stream-of-consciousness techniques like "automatic writing" and other methods, which were similar to Jung's suggestions for active imagination. There seems to have been very little direct contact between Jung and the Dadaists, although he attended a conference in Ascona at which some future Dadaists were present (Dachy, 1990). The remarkable coincidence is that Dada was founded in 1916 in Zürich where Jung was formulating his ideas on active imagination. It is possible that one or two of his own students may have attended Dada meetings.

The Dadaists and Surrealists were enormously attracted to dream imagery. Ironically, they were inspired by Freud and psychoanalysis rather than the analytical psychology of Jung. Their creative energy went into elaborating dream images rather than reductive attempts to penetrate their meaning. In this there was an affinity with Jung's suggestion to "dream the dream onward".

These parallel initiatives, one in the *avant-garde*, the other in analytical psychology, offer a clue to understanding an important paradox. How can it be that years of dedicated and intelligent research into the pictorial representation of inner states can lead to a number of important insights, which appear to be substantiated for a clinical working environment, and yet which cannot be relied upon for other situations? Susan Bach clearly believed that certain pictorial configurations such as the number of branches on a tree or anomalous use of colour could be translated into definite diagnostic or prognostic indications. Edward Adamson may be remembered for saying, when showing examples of patients' art work, that the portrayal of large areas of black and red in a painting should be regarded as some kind of danger signal, possibly of impending suicide.

It is always difficult to grasp the essentials of another's way of working, even within Jungian circles. Thus, while one may respect the finding that a conjunction of certain colours in a painting may *in certain circumstances* indicate grounds for alarm, it is very difficult to accept the idea of this, or any similar finding, applying outside a clinical situation. Such a generalization, if understood literally, would represent a most unsettling message to the individual and an intolerable restriction on artistic freedom.[1] We have to remember instead that certain pictorial configurations have symbolic significance and, depending upon the circumstances, might be acted out in a particular way. Susan Bach (1990, p. 7) acknowledges the work of Hans Prinzhorn (1922), whose researches into a vast collection of paintings by the mentally ill failed to identify specific or universal pathological images. In appreciating her work

---

[1] It is very important in this context to make use of a comparative method. Susan Bach was able to demonstrate detailed and precise differences between the pictures drawn by a healthy child and an ill one. See chapter 20 in *Life Paints Its Own Span* [Editor].

there must be, crucially, a recognition of the special context of potentially life-threatening situations in which she conducted most of her research. At times Jung seemed very clear that the same pictorial content has a different meaning according to who paints it. He recognized that the practice of Alchemy could be understood as a vain attempt to produce literal gold, or as a deep inner process of transformation. Jung drew our attention to the cross-cultural prevalence of archetypal images, but he knew that we also have to attend to the idiosyncrasies of personal circumstance. As I see it, there can be no other way of reconciling the integrity of one person's findings with another's and the fact that neither may hold true literally for all situations. One might say that it is a question of whether or not the relevant archetype is constellated in a given situation.

Susan Bach tells us that she developed an interest in the use of spontaneous paintings in the consulting room of a Jungian analyst. [1] This led subsequently to her participation in a "study group" at Netherne Hospital, Surrey. Diane Waller (1991) writes of this period that Edward Adamson, a former commercial artist with no previous psychological background, was invited to set up a free-painting group at Netherne following some post-war experiments with "group therapy" for ex-servicemen with severe neurotic problems. This was the group with which Susan Bach was associated and which from the beginning had research objectives. Waller quotes Dr. Cunningham-Dax, one of the psychiatrists involved in this project at Netherne Hospital:

> … an army sergeant had organised free painting there and Sybil Yates, an analyst with Freudian training who had been at the Tavistock, Mrs. Bach, a Jungian and I went there. When I returned to Netherne the staff were enthusiastic and Dr. Freudenberg, with many cultural interests, Dalberg, with a wide European experience, and Reitman who had been at the Maudsley before the war, all supported the project. Fortunately we were able to build a studio and gallery. Reitman told us about Edward Adamson, who was then a commercial artist and I persuaded the committee to employ him. I don't remember the timetable but he agreed to a number of principles which we laid down for him, especially that he was to stimulate and receive, not to teach, not to analyse, but observe and never to touch the patients' paintings. (Waller, 1991)

Thus Susan Bach was involved in a pioneering venture which contributed to the formation of ideas about the therapeutic use of art in Britain. From her contact with Jung and other therapists she had some psychological understanding, but her own skills developed in a different and perhaps unique way. In working with seriously ill children she adopted some of the guiding principles of the art project at Netherne Hospital, like promoting "spontaneous expression" with no teaching and minimal interference with the creative process, but neither the process nor the pictures which resulted were of interest as primary therapy. For her, the

---

[1] In the Preface to *Life Paints Its Own Span*, Bach tells us that her own collection of spontaneous drawings began in 1936. The child's drawing mentioned on p. 7 was collected in a school in Germany [Editor].

value was in the information they conveyed about the condition of the young patients. Despite the vividness and poignancy of much of this imagery, questions about "art" scarcely came into formal evaluation of the work. This may have been partly as a result of the overriding psychiatric concerns in the situation and partly out of a developing ethos in which there was a need to reassure patients that they were not expected to produce conventionally "artistic" pictures. This, however, is a subtle matter, since the methodology was more to do with the avoidance of preconceived artistic stereotypes, thereby allowing the patients maximum freedom of expression, rather than a denial of all aesthetic relevance or understanding. Edward Adamson, who worked with Susan Bach on the same project at Netherne Hospital, came from an art background:

> I believe that anyone who wishes to do this type of work should, first and foremost, be an artist. He holds the quiet authority of his vocation and can give a professional welcome to individual expression. The artist is uniquely placed to embrace the enigma of commencing a journey to an unknown destination. He can search without knowing what he is looking for, yet recognize his quarry the moment it appears .... The hospital artist's main role is to be a catalyst who allows the healing art to emerge. (Adamson, 1990)

A question arises as to what extent "the healing art" is dependent upon artistic understanding. In 1971 Irene Champernowne, who knew Adamson, and herself furthered substantially the development of art therapy in Britain, described Art and Therapy as an *uneasy partnership* (Champernowne, 1971; emphasis mine). Champernowne, at the Withymead Centre in the early 1950s, pioneered the technique of talking to a patient in the language of that person's picture, thus entering into its metaphor rather than overtly interpreting it psychologically. This was a distinct stream of Jungian therapy which proved highly influential upon the development of art therapy in Britain (Waller, 1991; Edwards, 1978; Stevens, 1978). It was also perhaps a more fundamental link with Jung's involvement in unconscious imagery. Irene Champernowne had shown some of her own inner pictures to Jung. One of these paintings is reproduced in his *Flying Saucers* monograph (Jung, 1958). She became a friend of Edward Bennett who had presented images by his own patients for Jung's comment at the Tavistock Lectures in 1935 (Jung, 1968). She also worked analytically in Britain with Jung's former assistant and colleague, H.G. Baynes, who was particularly interested in Jung's insights into unconscious imagery. Diane Waller writes of Irene Champernowne:

> She felt that she learned about art therapy for the first time from Baynes, and his *Mythology of the Soul*, a comprehensive demonstration of the combination of analytical psychology with art, became a kind of bible for her. His work also influenced her at Withymead, where she saw a clear distinction between the role of art therapist and that of psychotherapist: the art therapist would help the patient to *produce* the pictures but it was the psychotherapist who would enter into the deeper meaning of the work with the patient. Irene was inclined to refer to the art therapist as a "midwife" in the process. (Waller, 1991)

There is an obvious sympathetic link between the idea of the art therapist as a "midwife" and Susan Bach's perception of the "hospital artist" who was a facilitator rather than a therapist as such. However, it was definitely the case at Withymead that the art therapist could sometimes become the *primary* therapist for a particular person. This extension and deepening of the art therapist's role has led to the move in recent years to change the name of the discipline from "art therapy" to "art psychotherapy".

On what grounds might the case be made for giving attention to the language and values of art in a therapeutic setting? Perhaps because the practice of art represents a paradigm or analogue for inner processes of transformation. Susan Bach was able to perceive this very clearly, although the transformations she observed were usually towards closely impending death. Jung saw this too in the paintings of certain patients, whose imagery faded and wilted in anticipation of the end of life. However, just as it was Jung's great discovery that the practice of alchemy could afford an experience of profound life-affirming change, so too he realized that amplifying images by putting the imagination to work symbolically could offer the individual an increased sense of opportunity, choice and completeness.[1]

Symbolic material is, as Jung pointed out, always greater than any one interpretation. A symbol cannot be emptied out by explanation. This holds true in art as well as in psychology. The history of art lecture, as Gombrich declared, could as well teach psychologists something about symbols as a lecture by a psychologist can offer certain insights about art (Gombrich, 1965). Making or studying images from the unconscious almost always leads to a hermeneutic process of association and elaboration. Investigations based upon successive approximation are essential to dream work and also to creative activity. Furthermore, our personal orientation to the individuation process must depend upon something very like an aesthetic instinct. At different times Jung referred to the possibility of a "creative instinct", sometimes to a "religious instinct" and latterly to an "instinct for individuation". These formulations could suggest that our aesthetic sense may inform perceptions of "rightness" at a deep archetypal level.

References

Note: CW refers to the Collected Works of C.G. Jung, Bollingen Edition.

Adamson, E. (1990) *Art as Healing*. Coventure, London.

Bach, S.R. (1990) *Life Paints Its Own Span: On the Significance of Spontaneous Pictures by Severely Ill Children*. Switzerland: Daimon Verlag.

Baynes, H.G. (1940/1969) *Mythology of the Soul*. Rider.

Champernowne, H.I. (1971) Art and Therapy: an Uneasy Partnership. In: *Inscape*.

Dachy, M. (1990) *The Dada Movement, 1915-1923*. New York: Rizzoli/Skira

[1] This statement neatly encapsulates some of the aims of the Omega Foundation; see the Preface [Editor].

Edwards, M.P. (1978) Art Therapy in Great Britain. In: *The Inner Eye*. Museum of Modern Art, Oxford.

Edwards, M.P. (1989) Art, Therapy and Romanticism. In: Gilroy, A. and Dalley, T. (Eds) *Pictures at an Exhibition*. London: Tavistock/ Routledge.

Gombrich, E.H. (1965) The use of Art for the study of Symbols, *American Psychologist*, 20.

Jung, C.G. (1922) The Transcendent Function, CW VIII

Jung, C.G. (1932) Picasso. In CW XV. Also: Jung, C.G. (1966/1984) *The Spirit in Man, Art and Literature*. London: Routledge.

Jung, C.G. (1958) Flying Saucers: A modern Myth. In CW X.

Jung, C.G. (1963) *Memories, Dreams, Reflections*, Routledge, London.

Jung, C.G. (1968) *Analytical Psychology: Its Theory and Practice. The Tavistock Lectures*. Routledge and Kegan Paul, London.

Prinzhorn, H. (1972) *Artistry of the Mentally Ill*. New York: Springer.

Stevens, A. (1978) *The Withymead Centre: A Jungian Community for the Healing Arts*. London: Coventure

Waller, D. (1991) *Becoming a Profession: The History of Art Therapy in Britain, 1940-82*. London: Routledge.

12

Displaced Qualities of God as a Cause of Human Illness

by Susan R. Bach

In the following communication,[1] I would like to introduce you to an idea which, during the last few years, has emerged from my analytical work. The longer I was living with it, the wider the field of its application seemed to become. Although it thus appears to be capable of far wider use, I will here limit myself to the analytical field of Jungian psychology from which it grew.

One of the underlying causes of illness, very often physical as well as psychological, can be found in what I call "displaced qualities of God". This underlying pattern helps me to see the rightful protest of the psyche, which is so often at the core of a symptom, as well as to see a possibility for adjustment, for a more healthily felt and fuller life, and, in the best of all possibilities, for a cure and healing. But I am shy of these words.

There is no doubt that all of us who have been breathing in the air of the long-established Jewish-Christian tradition are somehow familiar with the qualities of God, such as the Creator and Ruler of the world and universe, as the Almighty, as the God of justice, mercy and truth – qualities as set out in the Old Testament (Ex. 3:46ff).

These divine qualities, if not securely fixed and held for us in a conception of God's totality, leave their numinous place and, so to speak, try to find a home, attach themselves to any, even the most inappropriate container or object, situation or institution. It is as if the need for recognition is unseveringly connected with these attributes, and through any means, good or evil, they will force us to become once more aware of them, as if in a desperate attempt to be returned to where they belong. Hence if a person, no more recognising the absolute, God-like character of these attributes, identifies themself more or less totally with one or more of them,

---

[1] This paper was originally read to the Analytical Psychology Club, London, 14th May 1956 and then intended for wider publication, which somehow never happened. This version of the paper has been edited by R. Goldstein.

then the person will be invaded, inflated or depressed; at any rate threatened and, in the worst of cases, overwhelmed by them. Such displaced qualities of God can play havoc in people.

This problem has been known right through human history – think of what the Greeks described as *hubris,* and of what in the Middle Ages was called possession. The question is: whether our time might be specially prone to such displacements, to such a disorder. At any rate, it needed the discoveries of modern psychology to give us insight into, and consciousness of, the energy pattern of the totally upset psyche, as well as the scientific language and imagery to describe, investigate and comprehend the processes involved, thus enabling us to relate anew to the values involved, and to ask afresh for the meaning of it all.

Once I had become aware of these different aspects of what seems to me a deep cause of human disturbances, the material seemed to stream in from my daily work, both from the psychic and the physical side of illness. With that awareness of the possible cause underlying such illnesses, I do seem to get much more quickly to a more comprehensive understanding of the illness, and thus travel more directly to the possible root, as well as finding the potential bridgehead on the side of health, from which healing might take place.

I do not claim that the living material that spoke to me in a new way could not also be differently approached and evaluated, or that it could not usefully be interpreted in another way. But this conception can give the analyst a frame in which to work. It puts the individual problem into relationship with a basic human question, and gives the personal trouble a place and order of significance, within other basic or more important troubles. It gives the analyst the steadiness and a solid basis from which to work; it gives her the security that marks the region on which she treads and it puts the human problem in a setting in which the eternal may shine through.

So, apart from a possibly deeper understanding of the undercurrent of the actual problem, situation or symptoms that brought severely ill patients for treatment, this insight has helped me to stabilise him or her more quickly, or bring the very ill one to a psychic therapeutic layer of relative stabilisation, from which co-operative work can begin within the I-You relationship of Jungian analysis.

To put it in analytical language, what happens to a human being at such a critical moment, when a quality of God becomes displaced, is that he becomes identified or dissolved within one of the dominant archetypes. Instead of being reinforced, say by the mother- or by the father-archetype, guided by the archetype of order, supported by the saviour and rallied by the hero, the ego loses the sense of its own value, and thus its chance to humanise the archetype; the ego is swept off its own human and individual ground and is overwhelmed by the archetype, and the I-You relationship is abolished.

In interpreting qualities of God with the aid of Jung's conception of the archetypes, I want to avoid the error that the unconscious is taken for the divine, and God is taken for the conscious. We need to remember that what we call God holds such eternal qualities of the total psyche as humankind has become aware of. Whether this happens through revelation, insight, or through our modern scientific approach, seems to be of less importance than the fact that the qualities of God *have* come into consciousness, *have* been realised and are given their proper place, from which, once more, their beneficial influence can hold and enrich humankind. Moreover, there is a temptation to substitute technical language for the numinosity of that totality which we mean when speaking of God.

In the following, I will take you the way the attributes of God may have taken when they travelled from their secure place of totality to the human individual. By choice, I will use the words and images under which we grew up; that is, the language of the Bible.

One of the deepest human problems and difficulties – to relate without becoming identified – has found an expression and is (or so it seems to me) reflected in the biblical creation chapter, Genesis 1:26, in the words: "And God said, Let us [I suppose speaking to Earth] make man in our image, after our likeness", or, as verse 27 puts it, "So God created man in his own image, in the image of God created he him, male and female created he them. 28 And God blessed them." With this word, God has given humans the potential possibility of recognising the image of God, has endowed them with a heart-strengthening assurance of being created in His likeness. To feel that God has created us in His image, could fill us with the greatest joy, the most humble pride. It could take away one of people's deepest sorrows, still one of their deepest fears: to be alone, bereft, to live alone and to die, unrelatedly, and alone. It could fill us with peace because, if God has not only created you and me, but has created us in His image, that means with potentials towards Him, He has related Himself to me, I am related to Him, I am as near to Him in my possibilities as in every bit of myself. So there is nothing unrelated.

But while we may experience the profound joy of being carried and supported by this wonder, beware of what may happen when we do not relate it back to its source, when we forget that we have the ability to reflect the light, but we are *not* the light, that we have the ability to be moved by the spirit, but are not the spirit, when God becomes so remote that we cease to be able to relate to Him and thus, perhaps out of loneliness and despair, fall for the desperate need to identify with Him in one way or another.

When searching for other sources that may have led human beings even more to identifying with God's qualities, I was led to another biblical notion: Leviticus 19:2, "Ye shall be holy, for I the Lord, your God, am holy" – the word holy taken as 'whole' or 'complete' – I was shaken when I saw it rendered in Matthew 5:48 as: "Be ye *perfect* even as your father in heaven is perfect." The feeling of God-likeness and nearness to Him, instead of holding and supporting humankind, became thus a life-threatening, overwhelming shadow of expectation. We know from Jung what it took him and we know what it takes us to redress, re-translate, humanise the call and the longing of integration by becoming as *complete* as we can within our given lifetime while giving up, while sacrificing the hope of becoming perfect. For what could be our blessing can become our danger, what could carry us and give us wings, may defeat and even destroy us.

Here I present two examples from many possible ones of the trouble which one predicate of God, perfection, turning into perfectionism, has caused in a human mind and a human body.

173

The first of the two case histories will show the psychological aspect of this dangerous infiltration, the second the physical in a surgical case.

Before going into these two more detailed accounts, I will provide just a brief indication of the fields in which this conception has proved to be useful. To mention only a few headings: To expect oneself to know too much, to know all and everything, to become the all-knowing one, may just give us a headache. The change from the blessing of the all-seeing eye to the spying eye that is felt only as a fault-finder; the misconception of the Saviour for which I may remind us of Hitler – in other words, when God begins to fall under the shadow of His qualities the Devil may come in – these are a few examples of what displaced qualities of God may do in the human individual. The most marked examples of this are to be found in the mental hospital field. To mention just one: megalomania. Furthermore, divine qualities may be projected onto less and less personal containers, such as groups, institutions, ideologies, and 'isms'. A trade union, for instance, may from a useful and necessary organisation be made into an idol, an end in itself; or vegetarianism can take the place of a religion, even driving it.

Case History – Psyche

The first detailed example is that of a young girl in her early twenties, who came to me originally more for discussion and support than for deeper therapy. She was the second of three children; first a sister, then she, then a younger brother. The marriage of the parents was unhappy: the mother, a Roman Catholic of Latin temperament, an intelligent, energetic and imaginative person; the father, a Northern Englishman who, very friendly to the children, lived part of his life outside their home. The elder sister was his favourite.

According to the mother's feeling, her elder daughter had stolen the husband's heart from her. The mother had to bring out her own unlived and unloved feminine side in this daughter, and made her into a proper Eve, whereas the second-born, my patient, should become the independent woman, out of her mother's own unfulfilled wish to qualify as a teacher. In accordance with her mother's design, my young patient had indeed become a teacher when her father died.

After a period of intense analytical work we had done together, she felt that teaching in a nunnery, as she called her boarding school, was not her line. She wanted to get nearer to life and grow up with congenial people. Slowly the wish emerged that she might become a real young woman, and have a husband and possibly children of her own. After careful discussion, she decided to go in for secretarial training as a means of getting a job nearer to her true interest. She hoped to do it within half a year's time rather than the usual three years. So she moved to London and started in a secretarial college.

Soon, in connection with the analysis of an attack of *asthma*, it came out that she was silently giving up the hope of ever becoming a good secretary; she did not reach the expected speed in shorthand and typing. This was a serious hitch in her endeavour to free herself.

There were two opposite sides of her speed problem in her personal realm; the impossibility of ever reaching the enviable achievements of her admired sister, who was always ahead of her, and, in its negative aspect, the fear of being overwhelmed by speed, of losing control, in connection with her brother. This brother, his mother's favourite, had a motorcycle and was driving it recklessly, often with her on the pillion seat, and in an awful recurrent dream of hers, he killed himself in an accident.

Here we are reaching archetypal ground. Speed is one of the predicates of God. Man's endeavour to overcome the boundaries of time and space by speed, although it has often helped him to reach far beyond his erstwhile limitations, if unrelated, if not serving a higher purpose, when becoming a goal in itself, often brings about self-destruction of mind and body; it spells disaster. Unfortunately, the girl's nightmare dream came true. Driving his motorbike at terrific speed, her brother crashed to his death.

After we had found how her speed problem was related to her brother, she was able to go back to the secretarial training. To my surprise, however, she was still not up to doing her shorthand and typing at the speed expected by her very understanding teacher.

When, in this difficult work, I come to a moment where I notice that on the personal, reductive level, the necessary movement and the needed release cannot be brought about, I look for the "below" and the "beyond". I search for an attachment or support on the collective, on the supra-personal, and on the macrocosmic level. In the case of a woman in such a situation I may look for misunderstood so-called "animus" qualities, or, on the highest level, a displaced quality of God, and see what may happen when her predicament is linked up with this conception.

So I asked my young patient once more why she thought she had to be first. Was it not good enough to be second? She said, "Oh, no, I could not give up, I want to be first." Asked whether it was such a nice thing to be first, she did not have the feeling really that it always was, but she was driven. I linked this up with my insight into what I have seen the Absolute is doing when it has no home. But before I would try to span this bridge from the individual to the beyond, the Absolute, I would once more check up on the personal level. So I took her problem to the Here and Now of the consulting room including myself, and we played being at the college. I asked if she should try to say to herself, "I will do as well as I can." She answered, "I was always told by my mother 'you can only do what you can', but what she *really* meant was that you were expected to be perfect." Now when this word came, I knew I was on the right track. She was burdened by her mother's expectation of perfection. I said, "Have you noticed when you have no doubt, when you can use all you have learned without driving yourself?" So I tried to reduce the absolute expectation and the absolute quality of speed by relating her shorthand and typing to her hope of making *practical* use of it. She said she had no doubt she would become a *good* secretary, but it was that she had to be a perfect secretary. So I suggested, "just try to recollect when you are good at writing – there may be a way you haven't realised when you can be very good indeed." To the delight of my heart, she said, "That's easy; once I have made a mistake I am alright." That means to say that, once she has made a mistake – has, as it were, become a fallen angel, become human – she can be as good as she can humanly be. In other words, if this girl has to carry God's perfection, as conceived of by her mother's world of principles, she inevitably has to fail, as would everyone else in her place. Trying to get a grasp of the girl's total situation, I asked myself how did such displacement come about in a potentially healthy individual? Her father who was to represent the outer security, the sheltering power at the back of her young growing self, had at first not been much in the house, became a non-entity and then left her altogether because he died.

The expectation of the protective, good father was transferred to the young brother, and he cast his life away, as she felt it. So there was only the mother, who then became the only carrier of the protective hand, the holder of the powers above us. The mother did not believe in anything other than that which she could control herself, her will-power. So the girl was confronted with a distorted image of God in her mother's, call it animus-ridden, concept of The Perfect, which was related to the highest value in its sinister aspect of a relentless and merciless principle, as perfectionism.

Actually I had met the mother before I saw the girl. She had been referred to me as a certified patient, from a mental hospital, for a three weeks' re-assessment because, in spite of years of severe mental illness, parts of the personality were still preserved. To show the deep-seatedness of the girl's problem, I give just a few details of the mother's life. As a child of ten, in desperate circumstances, she felt forsaken by God, called Him bad and cursed Him. She never got over the repudiation; either feeling guilty and awaiting punishment from almost every possible source, or wilfully and spitefully digging in her heels and taking her destiny – and later on unfortunately that of her family – into her own hands. Before returning to hospital, it had been the mother's wish that I should take on her daughter analytically and care for her.

Returning to my young patient, the moment when the spell of perfectionism was broken was the beginning of a period of re-education: to make her shorthand and typing speed a human affair, as well as dealing with other ramifications of this God-like quality. All the time we were battling with these difficulties in outer life, I had to be all she had not: her good mother, the protective brother, the caring father and the sister who lived so far away.

On the other hand, whilst waiting for the figures of her unconscious to come nearer the reach of her ego, I had to hold God's image for her. In this process of adjustment, *speed* finally became a helper, and perfection a guide. She gave herself some more weeks at the secretarial college and then took on a job requiring responsibility, versatility in human affairs as well as in office matters, rather than asking for high speed in shorthand and typing. I have continued to see her at intervals; her *asthma* attacks have become her guide when she strives too hard, and she has developed a sense of awareness when she is tempted to take on one of God's qualities, instead of being supported by them. Rather than reaching out for the Absolute, she is now doing what is possible for her.

Case History – Soma

On this occasion the body took over, to speak what the mind and body suffered, but could not express, so as to make it understood by the person in question.

The patient was in her mid-thirties, when she came to see me. She was the youngest of a family of three children, with an older brother and sister. The father was a General in the army of one of the great powers of Europe; the mother was a ballerina and a very cultured woman. The marriage was not happy; the parents separated and later divorced. The children grew up without set religion, under the care of two aunts and of a warm, although somewhat crude maternal grandmother. The small country of my patient's mother was seized by the great power her father served, thus reflecting and magnifying her parental conflict on the collective level.

The mother worked very hard to give her children the best education available and my patient felt that both her other siblings had betrayed her mother's brave attempt. She herself, willing to fight for her mother, her country, and humankind, regardless of cost to herself, became a courageous knight in carrying on the flame of the much-adored motherly spirit. There was a threefold load on her; her parents' conflict, her country and her own life.

The University became the high altar of all her young enthusiasm, devotion and joy of life – to serve knowledge was identified with truth, freedom and serving humankind. All became one there, all the more as she met her first love at the university; an older student. She herself was a lovable, courageous little stump; argumentative and embarrassing her friends and fellow-workers by not allowing any half-truth nor compromise, unable to give in if it came to inner convictions and principles, even where she wanted to and life required it. A certain rigidity in her walk and the way she would sit and carry herself gave the impression that there was something too upright and too straight – maintained by force of will rather than by the graces of nature.

Out of such rich analytical material, I will focus on three critical events in her life that seemed to reflect the same basic pattern. It is only more recently that I recognised the motive power underlying each of these crises as a displaced quality of God; in her case, a non-humanised relationship to the perfect, to the highest spiritual powers.

The first crisis was the problem of getting her straight with her fiancé. She called him the "Big One". He seemed to be the big brother, who brought all the fulfilment to her, all the backing, all the agreeing, which her non-existent father could not and her brother did not give her. So "Big One" became all the good, all the wonder in the world a man could be to a young loving heart. This is one of the moments when the highest values, which we may feel as contained, unrelated to God, may invade, or be projected upon, a human being most inappropriately fitted for it. "Big One" became identified with "The One" – he became an idol. Not only had this idol of a man infected her with venereal disease before she left her home country for England in 1939, but he had sent her a telegram just after the war was over saying that he had married another woman in the meantime. This telegram and its factual meaning I actually had to hold for her for a long time. She had to interpret it as a fake, sent in order to release her from her engagement with him, so that *she* could start a new life over here in England. I had to wait long and patiently, before she was able and ready to carry the disillusionment. The sign that the right moment had arrived came from her unconscious, when one day she started to move her engagement ring up and down her finger. This silver ring had a medallion in its centre. Next session the clasp of the medallion was open and nothing in it; she had lost her fiancé's photograph, his picture image.

After we had, up to a point, recovered his positive qualities – as we may say, the life-giving animus qualities – and when she had accepted that, in spite of it all, her meeting him had been a blessing, she could ask to have the telegram back, acknowledge its factual reality and burn it in my presence. It no longer held vital values for her and so it could go up in flames, could be returned to earth and ashes.

After a necessary and very successful branching out in her special field of work and in her social life over here, the next crisis occurred. With great pain, she told me how, after all these years of hoping to be reunited with her fiancé and her home country and making a home of her own, she had met a woman colleague and shared rooms with her. This friend of hers was well rooted in England, but very lonely and unhappily related to her feminine side, adopting a masculine haircut and style of dress. The need for making a home drew them together, and there was a temporary complementary attraction, which led to a substitute sexual relationship on a regressive level. The feelings of guilt, the sense of humiliation at allowing herself to be seduced, were immense. This time she herself had failed to live up to *her* sense of perfection and it nearly broke her. Courageously, she tried to build up a place of her own. Distance and her regressive, stubborn self-reliance prevented the desirable analytical support, so that I did not see her for quite some time.

I would like to say here that I regard body and mind as great friends, as perhaps the oldest and best marriage relationship one may find, where the one takes over in a case of emergency – and only then – what the other cannot do at that particular moment. In other words, the body will speak when, for some deep reason, the soul is unable to express itself in its joy or pain, or unable to bear it, and the other way round.

This seems to have happened with her. The next I heard was a telephone call asking me on her request to come to the surgical ward of a general hospital, as she was about to undergo an operation. For some time she had developed pain in her lower back, which was finally diagnosed as a slipped disc at the junction of the lower vertebrae and upper sacrum, which did not yield to physiotherapy, nor to other physical manipulations. So it was decided to replace it by manipulation under anaesthetic.

Being so afraid of going under the anaesthetic, which stood for going into the unknown, for letting go, she had to make sure that I would be there to hold her and to receive her back when she came round. The replaced disc slipped back again, and a few days afterwards she was operated on.

After her discharge from hospital, and feeling better, she was quite clear about one thing – she wished to leave London and take a job elsewhere, to make a clean break and start afresh. Without consulting me, under-estimating how much of her inner unresolved problems she would carry with her, she got tempted by a very attractive job, half academic, half in the practical field, at one of the growing younger universities. This would all have been very wonderful had not the man in charge had great shortcomings; a brilliant persona reflecting some of her father's qualities – in his intimate circle he was nicknamed "the window dresser". For a year I only heard from her by letters. She put all her hopes and enthusiasm into this work. Fearing the day when she would wake up and see the other side of this new medallion-figure, I held my heart.

Then one day I had a long distance call: she would be in London in two days, could I see her urgently over the weekend, before she would have to see the surgeon once more. The same symptoms had started all over again and she was in great physical pain. When she came I heard of her immense disappointment in her job. Instead of being supported by the professor, she felt called upon to cover up and carry his shortcomings, his "sins" as she put it. Coinciding with this disappointment, she told me the pain in the small of her back had reappeared. She became less and less able to move, to walk, to sleep. In her despair, she had fixed an appointment with the surgeon who had operated on her before, and then thought she should see me first.

By then, I had won greater insight into displaced qualities of God as a possible root of human illness and I thought I could see a link between her physical condition and her inner problems. By now it was clear, even to her, that she had taken on too much work, too much responsibility, a weight which was not hers to carry. As she is an intuitive and clear-minded person, with a long and good relationship to me, I could go directly into letting her translate University as *universitas*, meaning the whole, the whole of knowledge represented by a corporation of scholars and students. She could then see that she had tried to make this university a temple in the service of absolute truth and absolute knowledge, with her professor as a god, or high priest in the middle of it. She had projected divine totality into her university and had taken on the inhuman task of carrying it herself. Under this burden she had broken down, seduced by perfection. Avoiding biblical language for it is not hers, I could remind her of Atlas trying to carry the world on his shoulders and she could see the point.

Next morning, she rang me up and said very angrily – she has a wonderful sense of humour – "Damn you, I should have seen my surgeon first and you afterwards. You see, much of my pain is gone, I slept the whole night through. What shall I tell him? What did I come to

London for? I don't even know exactly the place where the silly trouble is." I said, "Don't be too sweeping, go and see him and let me know."

The surgeon suggested another operation, but advised her to wait for three weeks and warned her of the danger of recurrence, even after a second operation. I saw her twice more. With the help of a magnificent dream, we came to the point where she would really try and give back those responsibilities to where they belonged and only take on her own responsibilities, including herself and caring with all her might for, as her dream put it, the paralysed and frozen part of her non-life that needed her maternal warmth and devotion.

A second operation has not been needed and her pain has stopped. In the following two years, I only had an occasional letter.

In summary, this part of her story showed us what a displaced quality of God, in this case perfection, did to a human being and her body structure. This courageous woman nearly broke down under the impact of accepting that her fiancé, for reasons unknown to us, had caught venereal disease, and later on, we do not know why, had married another woman. It needed great care and skill to help her to see that she had expected him to be the carrier of an *eternal* value and to take back what of it was hers. The next time she came up against the perfect was in expecting it of herself. So her pain re-appeared after she had slipped from her very upright and too rigorous moral standards (when she had the passing experience with her older woman friend), making up for it by even greater uprightness and rigidity.

I would say already then the body took over and reflected the slip in her morals with the slipped disc. Finally, in her hope and effort to bring to fulfillment the university as the place of places, and when her idolised professor did not fulfil her expectations, she even took on the burden of the universe and broke down under it.

With the strange "law of the repetitive series", within the following weeks, I had referred to me two more professional women suffering from slipped discs, both leading people in their professions, both in the grip of principles, both with a bad or unclarified father relationship, and suffering from all its consequences, both with a marriage that had broken down because of, for short, inappropriate or too high expectations on both sides (in both cases very likeable people, the relationship to whom could be re-established on a basis of friendship). Both were immobilised when I met them first. I am happy to say that, after intense analytical treatment, both are well without the need for operations and have now taken up their work in a new way – as one of them put it, as if a new lease of life was granted her. Naturally, it took quite some time and immense care to re-relate them more humanly, both to their body and to the spiritual world.

I cannot emphasise too much that the factual knowledge, even in great detail of the above course of events and the ability to convey this complex cause and effect to the sufferer, does not effect a cure, but having this knowledge inside, and using it, helps the sufferer to modify his attitude and approach in carrying out day to day actions. It needs long and constant practice and experimenting with this new attitude to life's tasks.

The age-old problem of relating without becoming identified, without being dissolved in the identification, is a situation well known to all of us; one may over-identify with one's parents, one's child, one's husband, one's wife, one's friend, with a teacher, a famous writer or a favourite film or television star; then, in a somewhat different sphere, perhaps, with one's household or business, and still more impersonally, with one's political party, or any favourite 'isms'. In this chapter, we have been looking at this problem in a different sphere, the sphere of values, the highest of which, the totality of which we conceive in the idea of God. After describing some living experiences (that, in one way or another, may not only be those of a few people called patients, but could be our very own), I would now put the question in front of us; what is an answer, or our answer, to this profound and basic problem?

There have been helpful and encouraging answers to this question, not only for individuals, but for groups and peoples. To my deep regret, I cannot, in this paper, take you along the ways which, say Taoism has found, or Gnosticism, or the Cabbalah – the latter sending man in search of the golden qualities of God broken up in minute sparks and scattered everywhere. We might compare the insight to our knowledge of radioactive substances that, if used and applied in minute quanta, have a healing effect whereas, unguardedly or unknowingly exposed, will destroy life.

But is there a more courageous way, nearer to us today than these solutions of old? Although I may have noticed and observed many of the relevant factors – more than I could convey in this paper – I would not have been able to deal with them constructively, but for Jung's discoveries and findings on the lawful character of the basic processes within the psyche, which in their own order indicate a way to an answer, to a synthesis.

It would be a chapter in itself to attempt an explanation in fuller detail of how a positive, life-bringing relationship between the Absolute, the highest values of man, and the individual life can be brought about, through the recognition of these basic forces and processes in the mind and soul. But to put it in a nutshell, we have seen that divine qualities when invading a person – or expressed the other way round when a person becomes unconsciously identified with any one of them – can endanger that person. The excessive brilliance and fascination of divine qualities overshadows and more or less extinguishes the personal values, the self-valuation of the ego, and literally drives these values into the shadow from which they need to be rescued and reinstated. What happens when identification with a divine quality takes place is precisely that the overpowering influence puts the ego under the spell of the shadow. During what we call analysis, the task is to strengthen and support, in very severe cases even to substitute for the ego for a time, whilst simultaneously holding the values contained in the absolute for the injured human being. In this labyrinthine way of establishing or re-establishing the healthy ego feeling, the overpowering force will be reduced to its life-feeding measure. If all goes well in what we call the transference situation, the analyst will have to mediate and to humanise the archetypal, the numinous quality of God. Especially at such moments, the analyst herself needs to be aware of, and held by, what the priest may experience when mediating the dogma to the capacity of the individual who comes to him in his need. After the ego has recovered its sense of personal value, it will be the last turn of the journey called analysis when the ego, with its newly won security, can re-relate to that many-faceted whole which Jung has called the Self. Or to come back to the biblical example, if God has created us in His image, i.e. that we are able to reflect the divine in our human way, we can accept that, bearing the fingerprint of God on the individual soul, we can relate to Him without danger of becoming identified.

After the long way we have gone together, I would like to end on the very simple "I and You" situation of our daily life. I personally have found, when I come to a deadlock in an everyday position, in a personal or professional situation, I sit down with myself and ask whether I may not be under the power of an archetypal quality – whether I myself may not be under the shadow of a displaced quality of God. When I am in such a predicament, when I feel I have failed and cannot forgive myself, I have found that when I have given back to God what is God's and taken on the humanly possible in my life today, the tension or the cloud may lift. In short, when I have given back to God what is God's, I can do what is humanly possible for me in my life today.

List of Figures

Index

Susan R. Bach

Life Paints Its Own Span

On the Significance of Spontaneous Pictures by Severely Ill Children

The title of this book reflects the main themes from 50 years of Susan Bach's analytical work with spontaneous pictures and in her "blue room". In working with spontaneous pictures and drawings, she perceived the expression of deep connections between psyche and soma and learned that "it knows within us" when either healing or death is imminent.

Talking with Susan Bach about her work was inspiring and humbling and, drinking coffee as only she could make it, one felt deeply privileged to be studying with someone who brought so much intuition and intellectual understanding to the contemplation of the human psyche.

The humbling part of the conversation came from wondering how to move one's own work towards the paths she was opening up. The purpose of this collection of essays is to show how the work of connecting and finding meaning continues and advances, whether through pictures, objects, dreams or other images and myths.

The contributors have in common both a Jungian background and their having made distinguished contributions in their own specialities.

Part I (Text): 208 pages
Part II (Pictures, with over 200 color illustrations): 56 pages, ISBN 3-85630-516-5

C.A. Meier

Healing Dream and Ritual

Ancient Incubation and Modern Psychotherapy

C.A. Meier calls for modern psychotherapy to honor the role that the dream has played in the healing process, from ancient times to the present. (168 pages, ISBN 3-85630-510-6)

Healing Dream and Ritual is one of the most significant and lasting witnesses of how far beyond immediate psychology the implications of Jung's work stretches. This book is, in my feeling, as important for today's healers as was the early work of Paracelsus to the redirection of medicine in the Renaissance. – Sir Laurens van der Post

Ann Belford Ulanov

The Wizards' Gate – Picturing Consciousness

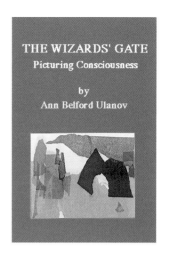

What do we do with the All, the Vast, the Radiance that stands steadfastly behind and through the near and the familiar? We make pictures – primordial images of the primordial. In this new book, adapted from the distinguished Hale Lectures, the author presents case material from a woman's wrestling with death, showing how inextricably mixed are matters theological and psychological. Author and reader embark on a joint adventure in religion and psychoanalysis.

(135 pages, color illustrations, ISBN 3-85630-539-4)

Alan McGlashan

The Savage and Beautiful Country

Alan McGlashan presents a sensitive view of the modern world and of time, of our memories and forgetfulness, joys and sorrows. He takes the reader on a safari into regions that are strange and yet familiar – into the savage and beautiful country of the mind. No "cures" are offered, but we are provoked to reflect on our roles and attitudes in the contemporary world jungle.
(228 pages, ISBN 3-85630-517-3)

Alan McGlashan conveys a poetic vision which has more to do with life as it can be lived than all the experiments of the laboratory psychologist or the dialectic of the professional philosopher.

– The Times Literary Supplement

A highly provocative work, filled with astonishing and exciting insights about the less rational aspects of man, but communicated to the intelligent layman in an engagingly informal manner.

– Library Journal

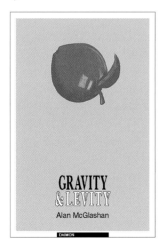

Alan McGlashan

Gravity and Levity – The Philosophy of Paradox

This book heralds a breakthrough in human imagination, not a breakthrough that may take place in the future, far or near, but one that has already occurred – only we may not have noticed it. Life, as the author shows, is open-ended and full of paradoxes. Its principles cannot be understood by logic and causal reasoning. We can only come to terms with life if we accept that there is no final answer to it and that adjusting to life's natural rhythm is the key to finding release from the horrors and problems around us.
(162 pages ISBN 3-85630-548-3)

Talking with Angels – Budaliget 1943

A document transcribed by Gitta Mallasz

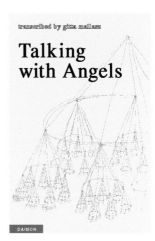

Budaliget 1943: A small village on the edge of Budapest. Three young women and a man, artists and close friends are gathered together in the uneasy days before Hitler's armies would destroy the world as they knew it. Seeking spiritual knowledge, and anticipating the horrors of Nazi-occupied Hungary, they met regularly to discuss how to find their own inner paths to enlightenment. One June afternoon, the meeting is disrupted when Hanna calls out, "Be careful, it is no longer I who speak!" Her friends do not recognize her voice now or later, when she speaks in other voices, each directing a specific message to one of the four. For 17 months, with the world locked in a deadly struggle for survival, the four friends meet every week with the spiritual beings they come to call their "angels"; Gitta Mallasz takes notes, the protocols which form this book, along with her commentary. The angels' message of personal responsibility is as meaningful and as urgent today as it was for its initial recipients half a century ago. (474 pages, ISBN 3-85630-564-5)

Yehezkel Kluger

A Psychological Interpretation of RUTH

with a companion essay: *Standing in the Sandals of Naomi,*
by Nomi Kluger-Nash

The biblical Book of Ruth is a love story, apparently personal and simple – of love between women and between man and woman – told in poetic imagery and style. Barely hiding within this immediate beauty are the archetypal depths which reveal nothing less than the eternal mystery of a love which brings about redemption and individuation both personal and transcendent, human and divine. Dr. Kluger wrote the original interpretation as part of the requirements of the first graduating class of the Jung Institute in Zürich. He later updated his work, but the thesis remains the same: the return of the feminine principle in the Bible. To this end, he examines the fate and role of the feminine as "she" travels from ancient times through various goddesses to the person of Ruth, and her destiny as restoring the original totality of masculine and feminine in equal, interacting, balance.

In counterpoint to the scholarly style of her father – while in unison with his interpretations – Nomi Kluger-Nash has written a woman's subjective reactions to the story of Ruth, Naomi and Orpah. To this associative style she brings further amplifications from Kabbalah into the meaning of these women who carry aspects, both light and dark, of the Shekhinah, the feminine presence of God. (230 pages, ISBN 3-85630-587-4)

ENGLISH PUBLICATIONS BY **DAIMON**

Susan R. Bach:
– Life Paints its Own Span
E.A. Bennet:
– Meetings with Jung
George Czuczka:
– Imprints of the Future
Heinrich Karl Fierz:
– Jungian Psychiatry
von Franz / Frey-Rohn / Jaffé:
– What is Death?
Liliane Frey-Rohn:
– Friedrich Nietzsche
Yael Haft:
– Hands: Archetypal Chirology
Siegmund Hurwitz:
– Lilith, the first Eve
Aniela Jaffé:
– The Myth of Meaning
– Was C.G. Jung a Mystic?
– From the Life und Work of C.G. Jung
– Death Dreams and Ghosts
Verena Kast:
– A Time to Mourn
– Sisyphus
Hayao Kawai:
– Dreams, Myths and Fairy Tales in Japan
James Kirsch:
– The Reluctant Prophet
Eva Langley-Dános:
– Prison on Wheels: From Ravensbrück to Burgau
Mary Lynn Kittelson:
– Sounding the Soul
Rivkah Schärf Kluger:
– The Gilgamesh Epic
Yehezkel Kluger & Nomi Kluger-Nash:
– A Psychological Interpretation of RUTH
Paul Kugler:
– Jungian Perspectives on Clinical Supervision

Rafael López-Pedraza:
– Hermes and his Children
– Cultural Anxiety
Alan McGlashan:
– The Savage and Beautiful Country
– Gravity and Levity
Gitta Mallasz (Transcription):
– Talking with Angels
C.A. Meier:
– Healing Dream and Ritual
– A Testament to the Wilderness
Laurens van der Post:
– The Rock Rabbit and the Rainbow
R.M. Rilke:
– Duino Elegies
Miguel Serrano:
– C.G. Jung and Hermann Hesse, A Record of Two Friendships
Susan Tiberghien:
– Looking for Gold
Ann Ulanov:
– The Wizards' Gate
– The Female Ancestors of Christ
Ann & Barry Ulanov:
– Cinderella and her Sisters
Erlo van Waveren:
– Pilgrimage to the Rebirth
Harry Wilmer:
– How Dreams Help

Jungian Congress Papers:

Jerusalem 1983: Symbolic and Clinical Approaches
Berlin 1986: Archetype of Shadow in a Split World
Paris 1989: Dynamics in Relationship
Chicago 1992: The Transcendent Function
Zürich 1995: Open Questions in Analytical Psychology
Florence 1998 – Destruction and Creation: Personal and Cultural Transformations (in preparation)

Available from your bookstore or from our distributors:

In the United States:

Continuum & Cassell
22883 Quicksilver Drive
Dulles, VA 20166
Phone: 800-561 7704
Fax: 703-661 1501

Chiron Publications
400 Linden Avenue
Wilmette, IL 60091
Phone: 800-397 8109
Fax: 847-256 2202

In Great Britain:

Airlift Book Company
8 The Arena
Enfield, Middlesex EN3 7NJ
Phone: (0181) 804 0400
Fax: (0181) 804 0044

Worldwide:
Daimon Verlag
Hauptstrasse 85
CH-8840 Einsiedeln
Switzerland
Phone: (41)(55) 412 2266
Fax: (41)(55) 412 2231
email: daimon@csi.com
http://daimon.webjump.com